SEASONED SERVANTHOOD

The Key Ingredient for a Thriving Nation

Sally Mahihu

Table of Contents

Dedication

I dedicate this book to the entire Faith Evangelistic Ministry (FEM) fraternity. First and foremost, to the Founder, my Spiritual Authority and Mentor Rev. Teresia Wairimu, the Ministers and my fellow co-workers who have been very instrumental in teaching me how to serve, and because they reflect a lot of the experiences I have shared in this book.

Acknowledgement

First and foremost, I would like to thank God for giving me the ability, wisdom and grace to write this Book. Without His hand and divine directing, this book would not have been possible.

My husband **Ngari**, whose consistent unwavering and unconditional love and support throughout the writing of this book is beyond words.

My sons **Eric** and **Chris** who encouraged and kept cheering me.

I am deeply and immensely grateful for having God's best and finest Spiritual Authority and Prophet **Rev. Teresia Wairimu** who as stated elsewhere was a key catalyst in my writing this book. For her constant prayers and words of wisdom, for pushing me to rise above the mediocre. For calling out the gift of writing in me and for nurturing it faithfully. For writing me such a powerful foreword for this book which I certainly do not take for granted.

My sincere thanks and appreciation to **Her Excellency Madam Rachel Ruto,** who was also instrumental in the conception of this book and for her continued support and for cheering me on and constantly but gently reminding me that I needed to birth this book. I also thank her entire team and staff members who were also a catalyst to the conception of this book following the seminar that I conducted for them on this subject of servanthood.

I must pay honour to my late Dad **Chris Kahara** for affirming me throughout my life and instilling self-confidence in me, who would definitely have understood the content of this book because of his many years in the civil service.

To my editor **Dr. Mark Stibbe** whose professionalism and editing skills are unmatched and my friend Ann Jackson another promising writer for her inspiration and vote of confidence in me when I shared about this book.

My Publisher & Cover Designer Shadrack Radido of House Of Wealth Publishers whose passion for this book really fuelled and motivated me to forge on without losing momentum

To **Lucy N. Kimanzia** promising writer in her own right who was a great encouragement to me because of her enthusiasm about this subject and her deep insights especially with regard to the spheres and sectors of service which she is very passionate about.

To my assistant **Victor Mutahi Mwangi** who has walked this journey with me faithfully and diligently with an excellent spirit and dedication to the point where he knew portions of this book better than I and was always keen to ensure meticulous attention to detail and to encourage me when I became weary or momentarily lost focus. Also, to my typist and research assistants **Frida Wanjira** and **Tecla Karimi** whose commitment and dedication and the manner in which they committed to this work was beyond my expectations. To my entire team of staff in my law firm who obediently carried out their duties often without my supervision while I focused on my writing.

And to everyone else who contributed in one way or another to the physical creation and completion of this work.

Foreword

When I met Sally two decades ago, she was at the early stages of her walk with God, still a young lawyer, wife and mother and as she has served me in Ministry all those years, I have seen her grow tremendously both spiritually and professionally. She is a wise woman strongly gifted in speaking and teaching.

Sally rightfully refers to me as her Mentor and Spiritual Authority, because she has submitted and served under my Leadership in Church Ministry for those decades, I have known her, and she has allowed me speak into her life and nurture the various gifting within her.

This book on "**Seasoned Servanthood**" affects many of us in our capacity as Leaders and Servants because it reinforces the principle, that lest we have learnt how to serve and to do so faithfully, we cannot qualify to call ourselves Leaders, because good and true Leadership in essence, arises from good and true Servanthood. It is a reminder that our attitude even as Leaders should predominantly be an attitude of one serving those you are leading.

Perhaps, the scripture that stands out most significantly for me in relation to this book on the subject of Servanthood is *John 13:5-17* when Jesus washed his disciples' feet as a demonstration that He came primarily to serve, and that true greatness stems from an attitude and heart of Servanthood and humility.

Servanthood resonates deeply in my spirit because as a Prophet and Servant of God, my Call is all about service and Servanthood.

I began serving God from my early twenties and one of the most fundamental revelations I got even at that early age and stage of my Call, was that serving God and by extension serving His people is what I was born and created for.

It is a privileged position to be called to serve in any capacity and in the execution of your duties (whether in the church community, in the market place, and in the Nation generally), you must be conscious of the fact that you are fulfilling God's agenda and ultimately contributing to your Nation's growth.

Sally has done an excellent job by presenting the call to Servanthood in its depth and reality, capturing every aspect in an articulate and down to earth manner that makes Servanthood not only palatable but also easy to embrace and even desirable.

This book will change the lives of many people serving in the various spheres and sectors of influence because it will change many minds regarding Servanthood, giving a deeper understanding and providing many with the necessary motivation to rededicate themselves to this very noble Call, for our individual and corporate growth, because as Sally has correctly put it, *"Servanthood is a key ingredient for a thriving Nation."*

Rev. Teresia Wairimu Kinyanjui.

Director& Founder,

Faith Evangelistic Ministry (FEM).

Endorsement

Many books have been written on servanthood. This is a comprehensive piece of work that brings in an often-overlooked dimension which I believe is the bedrock of servanthood. This is the spirit of service. Servanthood has many times been misconstrued as service by the lowly in society. Oftentimes the mention of the word servant hood elicits feelings of undignified service among many. This book however clearly highlights the importance of dedicated service as a fundamental aspect of any prosperous society.

Sally meticulously summarizes valuable principles on which servanthood is to be founded. These she calls the 7P's. It is worth noting that this book addresses the critical subject of leadership as is related to intentional and impactful service. Similarly, the issues that are deterrent to service and servanthood are candidly elaborated. It is impressive that Sally has not only taught on this pertinent subject but has endeavoured to live the talk. This book is a handy asset for those who are committed to serving with relevance and for posterity.

Her Excellency,

Rachel Ruto,

Spouse of the Deputy President, Republic of Kenya.

Endorsement

"There are many books about leadership and management, as any visit to the relevant section of a large bookstore will show, but there are precious few books about the one indispensable mind set and practice that all organizations need to flourish, "Servanthood". An attitude of service leads to a lifestyle of service and a lifestyle of service leads to the discovery of your destiny in service. Without this value being deeply embedded in every heart and every part of an organization – including in the leadership – there will be no lasting success.

Sally Mahihu's book is therefore invaluable. By showing that the spice of servanthood is the key ingredient that needs to season every organization in every sphere of culture, she has served us a feast that will nourish and sustain us for a long, long time.

This is essential wisdom and should be required reading for everyone who seeks to serve their country, their company, their church

Dr. Mark Stibbe.

Introduction

Until I become active in Church as a born-again Christian some 28 years ago, I had never quite understood the concept of true Servanthood, and it soon became an area of great interest to me as I got magnetically drawn and immersed into the culture of Christian Servanthood.

Writing this book came from a deep interest on this intriguing subject. I was however amazed at the disturbing contrast between the attitude and culture governing service in the Church and the attitude and culture governing service in the non-church sectors and spheres. This disparity disturbed me so much that I was determined to delve deeper into this subject and find some answers, and I discovered that the main factor that causes this difference in culture and attitude is that whereas those serving in the church sphere have a very clear revelation that their service to man is primarily service to God, many of those serving in the other non-church, sectors and spheres may not consciously link or connect their service to man as being service to God.

My aim therefore in this book is to advocate very strongly that your service, whether within or outside the Church sphere, must be based on the premise that it is ultimately all to the glory of God. This is because you are serving where you are by the divine plan of God.

The specific incident that inspired me to write this particular book took place about two years ago when I got a request to give a half-day seminar titled 'Principles of Serving a Leader' to a team of staff members working for a Government Leader.

My first statement that captured their attention was *"How you serve your leader(s) in whatever sphere or sector affects the lives of millions of people for whom that leader is responsible. The higher the ranking of that leader within a nation and the greater the influence he or she commands, the more the lives he or she is responsible for."*

I went further to emphasize that anyone serving a Leader (and that Leader's Vision) in any sphere or sector has been carefully chosen for a very special purpose and assignment. It is not by chance or coincidence that you find yourself in such a position. Therefore, you need to appreciate the fact that you were chosen by God specifically for that task and assignment, even before you were conceived in your mother's womb.

Jer 1:15 – *Before I formed you in the womb I knew you, before you were born, I set you apart.*

I further explained that servanthood is a call that needed to be understood and walked in as it impacts directly on our individual destiny. This is because your servanthood directly impacts on your ability to fulfil the Purpose for which you were created and the Destiny to which you have been called.

To the glory of God, the principles I shared during that short seminar two years ago had such a significant impact on that team of staff members, that was beyond my expectations. It was actually some members in that team who challenged me, when they consolidated those principles, I had taught them into a "booklet".

My Spiritual Authority and Mentor, Reverend Teresa Wairimu who had recommended me for that seminar, immediately and very categorically, advised me to go beyond a "**booklet**" and expound this topic about Service and Servanthood into a concrete full-fledged book. I should mention that I was not at all surprised by her advice. Being a woman of great insight and intentional purpose, she has mentored and spoken into my life for many years and she had repeatedly told me, that there was a gift of writing within me that needed to be unleashed. The rest as they say is history because pursuant to that explicit and strong affirmation I embarked and concluded this book you are now reading.

This book covers every aspect of the concept of Servanthood which I have dubbed the 7P's. They include the **Principles** of a Servant (the core precepts upon which true Servanthood is founded namely the revelations, the elements and the choices); the **Persona** of a Servant (namely the character and competence of a Servant); the **Purpose** of service (namely the functions, attitudes and endowments of a Servant); the **Place** (namely the sphere, sector and position where a Servant is called to serve); the **People** that Servanthood will include (namely the different types of characters you will encounter in the course of your servanthood and the codes and terms of engagement you will need, to ensure you relate to them appropriately, including the critical relationship with the Leader(s) you will find yourself serving from time to time and the co-servants you will inevitably find yourself serving with); the **Process** of Servanthood (namely the tests and trials you will need to endure, the seasons you will have to grow through as well as the radical surgeries and refinements you must undergo to become a premium Servant); and finally the **Prize** (namely the rewards whether the external, internal or external that you will lay hold of for your faithful Servanthood).

This book also extends to every sphere and sector of service (such as the sphere of Politics and Governance, the sphere of Business and Economy, the sphere of Media, the sphere of Arts and Entertainment, the sphere of Education, the sphere of Family, the sphere of Church and the Community development sector) meaning that the fundamental tenets of service are more or less similar across the board.

I wrote this book because I am deeply persuaded that if we truly embrace the Call to true Servanthood in whichever sphere or sector, we are in we will thrive as individuals, families, churches, institutions, communities and ultimately as a Nation.

Adhering to the principles of faithful Servanthood will eliminate vices such as self-centeredness, selfish interests and selfish ambitions, self-serving motives and agendas, treacherous betrayals, vicious sabotages, fierce competition and bitter wrangles for power and positions. True Servanthood will also eliminate family conflicts, ethnic divisions etc. and greatly reduce mismanagement of resources, corruption, abuse of office and unethical dealings in the market place etc. because true Servanthood focuses on the welfare of others out of which our own welfare is guaranteed.

One of the other reasons that drove me to write this book was because I can personally testify that having served in the church sphere and more specifically in Faith Evangelistic Ministry and FEM Family Church as a co-worker for many years, I became deeply convinced that how we serve is very closely connected and related to how we ultimately fulfil our Calling and Destiny.

Perhaps another compelling reason for writing this book, is to give a correct portrayal of the concept of Servanthood as an honourable call, and to counter the negative connotations it has been associated and regarded with as a menial degrading chore. Once we understand the power and impact that true Servanthood has on a people and on a Nation, then our perception and paradigm towards it will shift, thereby making us more deliberate and effective in our service.

Beyond empowering readers who simply wants to learn and enhance their Call to Servanthood, this book is specifically detailed and structured in a way that makes it a reference and teaching material for any kind of institution and organization, governmental departments, schools and colleges, as well as Church groups where there is a need to revamp the spirit of Servanthood, for that sphere and sector to thrive and fulfil its vision and mandate.

When this book is used as a tool in the various sectors and industries it will instil a genuine and sincere desire to serve and to serve well and it will equip those serving towards unleashing their full potential. It is for this reason I have included questions at the end of each section to provoke group discussions, personal reflection and growth etc.

This book is therefore intended to provoke and challenge anyone who is in a serving capacity to adopt the precepts expounded here towards enhancing and improving their service not only for the benefit of those or that which they are serving but also for their personal fulfilment and benefit. It is intended to reveal that true Servanthood is part and parcel of our Calling and Destiny and the more we embrace and master it the more effective we become in fulfilling our Destiny.

My intended target audience is all those serving in whatever capacity and in whatever sphere or sector and at whatever level and rank of service, whether it be within family units, communities, churches, businesses, politics and governance, education and training, media, arts and entertainment etc.

As stated earlier my first real encounter with the concept of Servanthood came through my involvement in the church, and from my experience most Christians who are committed members of home-churches and fellowships, have more or less understood and embraced this concept of Servanthood and this book will simply re-enforce what they have already heard and are already practicing, yet I believe that the depth and detail in this book will still add much value to the church.

This book also targets those serving in Leadership positions or bearing the title of a Leader, because every one of us is a Servant in one context or another considering that even those who are the highest ranked Leaders in whatever sphere, whether it be a President, a King or Queen of a Nation, CEO's, Captains of Industries, Heads of Families and Communities etc. they are also serving the people they have been entrusted with, even as they are being served.

In other words, a Leader who does not have a Servant's heart and attitude or who does not consider himself or herself a Servant is bound to fall short. The most effective Leaders are Servant Leaders.

Even the spiritual Leaders such as the Pope, the Arch Bishops, the Prophets and Apostles etc. are serving God and the people of God even as they themselves are being served.

This book is therefore a must read for every person in whichever sphere of influence or walk of life, who seeks to master the art of service, and the noble Call of Servanthood.

The book starts off by laying a foundation about the Principles a Servant needs to internalize about Servanthood which include the core precepts upon which true Servanthood is founded because it is by firstly understanding this, that the other aspects of Servanthood will fall into place.

This Page Was Intentionally Left Blank

Chapter 1

YOUR PRINCIPLES AS A SERVANT LEADER

The Core Precepts Upon Which True Servanthood is Founded

"Servanthood is the only job vacancy God has for us."
~ T. D. Jakes

Chapter Outline

The 7 Resounding Revelations About Servanthood

1. A Realization
2. A Redefining
3. A Responding
4. A Resolving
5. A Recognition
6. A Rooting
7. A Relinquishing

The 7 Essential Elements of Servanthood

1. A Consensual Covenant
2. A Tested Trust
3. A Vibrant Vision
4. A Concrete Connection
5. A Common Goal
6. A High Honor
7. A Sacred Stewardship

The 7 Conscious Choices in Servanthood

1. To Serve Sacrificially (S)
2. To Listen Emphatically (E)
3. To Serve With Revelation (R)
4. To Be Vested In Servanthood (V)
5. To Pledge Allegiance (A)
6. To Serve & Remain Nameless (N)
7. To Serve By Remaining True (T)

INTRODUCTION

True servanthood is birthed through a series of the following: some resounding revelations, some conscious choices, and some essential elements which are the fundamental core principles upon which it is founded.

Serving in any of the following spheres may entail either having a position of leadership, and therefore embracing a servant model of governance, or it may entail you serving such a leader and their vision.

In the sphere of the Church, you may either serve in the highest office of a bishop, prophet, apostle, or as an armour-bearer, an assistant, or member of the congregation.

In the sphere of arts and entertainment, you may either serve as the main artist, musician or sports person, or you may serve such people, for example as a personal assistant, a bodyguard, or a driver.

In the sphere of business and the economy, you may either serve as the CEO or chancellor of the exchequer, or you may function as a personal assistant, manager, or administrative support team member.

In the sphere of politics and government, you may either serve as the head of state, governor, president, or you may serve as a deputy, an assistant or a secretary.

In the sphere of the media, you may serve in the capacity of a media owner - such as a newspaper mogul or TV producer - or in the capacity of a journalist or presenter serving people in such leadership positions.

In the sphere of medicine, you may either serve as the company CEO (for example, of a pharmaceutical corporation) or as a hospital director, or you may support these leaders as a clinician or a nurse.

In the sphere of family, you may either serve as the head of the family or as a housekeeper, postman, or gardener.

I want to propose to you in this book that the principles of servanthood - the characteristics, attitudes, heart, alignment and positioning - will be the same irrespective of the sphere in which you are serving. The only aspects that will differ may be the endowments, gifting, talents and skills required, as well as the giants to slay.

Furthermore, I want to show you that in every sphere, greatness is defined not by power, position and titles but by humility and servanthood. The "top dog" or "celebrity mentalities have nothing to do with greatness. We are at our best when we serve others and make a difference by doing so.

For Christians, the call to serve flows out of our identity, out of who we understand ourselves to be in Christ. When we adopt our role as servants of Jesus, we build relationships, we earn trust, and we transform lives.

The world is uncomfortable with the words "servant" and *"follower"* because they are felt to imply weakness, reflecting a docile and doormat function. But the word "servant" does not mean that the person is somehow diminutive. Servant is a title of honour.

Servants form the critical mass in any society and nation. Without followers, there would be no leaders. Serving has its own dimension of influence and is vested with great significance, as you will see throughout this book.

It is time to recapture the beauty of the word "servant" and to be captivated by the majestic idea of "servanthood."

There are few things more powerful than a servant heart and a volunteer spirit.

THE 7 RESOUNDING REVELATIONS ABOUT SERVANTHOOD

Opening Remarks

Discovering that you have a call to serve is a life-changing realization. When you decide to accept and embrace that call, it produces an irrevocable response, a clear redefinition of your life in which you now know your identity as a servant. This in turn produces a single-minded resolve to dedicate yourself fully to that call. From now on, you recognize God's delegated authority upon the leadership you serve, and you embrace your strategic rooting in the place and the sphere where you have been called. This involves you dying to self as you undergo your development into a premium, seasoned servant.

1. A REALIZATION

"The real voyage of discovery consists not in seeking new landscapes, but in having new eyes." (**Marcel Proust**)

A Realization is a Discovery

To "discover" is to find, locate, uncover, unearth something, either through a conscious search or through stumbling upon it unexpectedly. To discover is to acquire knowledge of something, gain insight into it, to learn about it, to unmask it, to experience an unveiling, or receive a revelation. "Discovery" implies a process beyond simply "finding" something; it suggests having to dig deep to unearth something valuable and precious, something beneath the surface, concealed only for the diligent to locate.

This can be a Sudden Discovery

Discovering your call can either be through a sudden realization or revelation, leading to a radical paradigm shift - a "Damascus

Moment," such as the one Saul had (Acts 9:1-22) when he became Paul. This will lead to a 180-degree turnaround from what you previously believed or understood your calling to be.

It can be a Gradual Discovery

This discovery can be a gradual realization over time, one brought about by undergoing experiences or processes that bring you to a full-blown understanding.

And Jesus, walking by the Sea of Galilee, saw two brothers, Simon called Peter, and Andrew his brother, casting a net into the sea; for they were fishermen. Then He said to them, "Follow Me, and I will make you fishers of men." They immediately left their nets and followed Him. **Matthew 4:18-22**

There can be a Magnetic Pull Towards Your Discovery

Once you discover the call to serve, you will then discern the vision you are to follow when you identify the vision bearer ordained for you. You will experience a constant magnetic pull towards that vision and vision bearer as a confirmation of your discovery.

"No discovery was first made without a bold guess." **(Isaac Newton)**

The Activation of Your Discovery

After discovery, there is an activation of gifts, talents and skills within you, confirming you have the raw competence, capacity and the ability to serve the vision and the vision bearer. Through time, those gifts, talents and skills are harnessed and sharpened to become more and more effective.

Your Keys of Discovery

Discovering your call to serve may be a purposeful act that will require you to apply yourself diligently and then use the keys for discovering your purpose. These keys are found through a concerted, deliberate effort involving an identification of what you love, what fires your passion, what calls forth and utilizes your natural aptitudes.

"The things you are passionate about are not random; they are your calling." (Fabienne Fredrickson)

Failure to Discover

The opposite of discovering something is the suppression of insight, revelation and understanding. This leads to your call remaining concealed and unfulfilled.

2. A REDEFINING

"Self-discovery is a process of knowing yourself and the beginning of all wisdom" (Aristotle).

The discovery of your identity as a servant leads to a radical paradigm shift

"You are no longer a slave but a son, and if a son, then an heir of God through Christ." **(Galatians 4:7)**

Self-Definition

Beyond the discovery of their call to serve, a servant must also acquire an understanding of who they are. As a true servant, you must come to know who you are according to your own definition, and not according to other peoples' definitions of you.

Self-Knowledge

More importantly, as a servant you must have a knowledge of who you are in Christ - meaning your position in Christ as a child of God.

Or do you not know that your body is the temple of the Holy Spirit who is in you, whom you have from God, and you are not your own? For you were bought at a price; therefore, glorify God in your body and in your spirit, which are God's. **(1 Corinthians 6:19-20)**

Self-Secure

As a servant, you must be confident in your identity because you cannot serve effectively if you are insecure. It takes a secure and great person to serve the vision of another.

"The best way to find yourself is to lose yourself in the service of others." **(Mahatma Gandhi)**

Servanthood is True Greatness

As a servant, you must come to a revelation that being a servant is a very noble call. It is a true sign of greatness in the eyes of God. The worldly view - that servanthood is lowly and demeaning - must be rejected as false.

"Servanthood transcended all that it was thought to be and became what it was never imagined to be." **(Ralph Waldo Emerson)**

No Celebrity Status

As a true servant, you must know and be secure in your identity and you must also remember that this position in life gives you no name, no celebrity status, no frontline recognition and no public accolades. You must take a low profile and securely remain under and behind the leadership you are serving.

Most assuredly, I say to you, a servant is not greater than his master; nor is he who is sent greater than he who sent him. **(John 13:16)**

Servanthood is Defined by Function and Purpose

Your call to servanthood is not defined by your position or title but by your purpose and function. It is what you do, and the purpose you fulfil, that is important.

Sonship with Servanthood

You must balance your sonship with your servanthood because if you serve without having a clearly defined identity, you will develop a slave mentality. Likewise, if you embrace your sonship without a spirit of servanthood, this will lead to a "spoiled brat" mentality. The perfect balance is being secure in who you are (a son or a daughter of God) and having a servant heart.

3. A RESPONDING

"It is in your moments of decision that your destiny is shaped." **(Tony Robbins)**

What we are talking about here is your irrevocable decision to respond, to accept and embrace the call to serve.

But Jesus said to him, "No one, having put his hand to the plow, and looking back, is fit for the kingdom of God." **(Luke 9:62)**

A Firm Decision

Beyond discovering that you have a distinct call to serve, and beyond defining the vision, you must then make a firm decision to embark on serving. As Jesus told his disciples, once you have made a commitment to follow, there can be no turning back to the more comfortable and self-serving life that you once enjoyed.

Suspend Your Own Agenda

As a true servant, you must be prepared to suspend your own agenda and serve the agenda of your leadership. This means that you must suspend your own vision and focus on your leadership's vision first. You must understand that this vision must be fulfilled first before you embark on fulfilling your own.

A Paradigm Shift

A servant will undergo a radical process of decision-making amounting to a paradigm shift. This is known as *an Elisha experience* - when you make a sudden decision on the spur of the moment, with no looking back. Your decision should not be a seasonal or temporary one, but long-term and irreversible.

And he left the oxen and ran after Elijah, and said, "Please let me kiss my father and my mother, and then I will follow you." And he said to him, "Go back again, for what have I done to you?" **(1 Kings 19:20)**

Decision Plus Action

Knowing and responding to the call must cause you to graduate to a place where you make a firm decision to embark on the call and take action to fulfil that call.

"A good decision is based on knowledge and not numbers." **(Plato)**

A Conscious Free Choice

Your decision to embark on the call to serve must be consciously and voluntarily made, not coerced by someone else.

A Costly Decision

Your decision may lead you to make sacrifices and to incur losses because it may disrupt your comfort zone and clash with the opinions of your loved ones.

"There is no decision that we can make that doesn't come with some sort of balance or sacrifice." **(Simon Sinek)**

Your Decision Will Empower You

Once you have made this radical, irreversible, sacrificial decision, you will be automatically empowered by your very ability to make that decision and this will greatly enhance and energize your servanthood.

4. A RESOLVING

"Success is about dedication. You may not be where you want to be or do what you want to do when you're on the journey. But you've got to be willing to have vision and foresight that leads you to an incredible end." **(Usher, American musician)**

This speaks of a single-minded resolve to dedicate yourself fully to that call.

A Total Dedication

Beyond discovering that you have a call to serve, and beyond defining your identity and being secure in it, and beyond making an irreversible decision to fulfil that call, as a true servant you must go a step further and dedicate yourself totally and fully to that call.

A Heart and Soul Matter

To dedicate yourself entails giving your time, energy heart and soul.

"Nelson Mandela, a better man, not a bitter man, made our world a better place in which to live. His life and leadership exemplify the highest courage, dignity and dedication to human liberation." **(Bernice King)**

So, his armour bearer said to him, "Do all that is in your heart. Go then; here I am with you, according to your heart." **(1 Samuel 14:7)**

This was Jonathan's armour-bearer demonstrating his total dedication to his master.

We too must be prepared to say that we will go where our leader is going, following them in a heartfelt and committed way. This is more than just an intellectual assent or an act of the will; it is a passionate allegiance to the leader and their cause/vision.

An Unwavering Resolve

To dedicate yourself means to be single-minded, fully focused and unswerving in your dedication.

A Conviction not a Convenience

Total dedication will require a confirmed commitment to serve in and out of season by conviction and not convenience, whether you feel like it or not.

A Physical, Mental and Emotional Involvement

Dedication makes a demand upon your mind, emotions, physical energy and time, requiring your total investment and involvement.

A love and Passion Affair

Dedication is birthed out of a deep passion and love for the leadership and its vision/cause.

A Service Devoid of Apathy and Laxity

The absence of dedication is laxity, apathy and indifference and a clear indication that you do not have what it takes to be a servant.

"Any job well done that has been carried out by a person who is fully dedicated is always a source of inspiration." **(Carlos Ghosn)**

5. A RECOGNIZING

This is the respectful recognition and acknowledgement of God's delegated authority upon the leadership you are serving.

Obey those who rule over you, and be submissive, for they watch out for your souls as those who must give account. Let them do so with joy and not with grief, for that would be unprofitable for you. **(Hebrews 13:17)**

The Legitimacy of Your Leadership's Authority

Beyond discovering that you have a call to serve, beyond defining your identity and being secure in it, beyond making an irreversible decision to fulfil that call, beyond dedicating yourself to the call, as a true servant you must go a step further and make a determined recognition and acknowledgment of who you have been called to serve, knowing that they are a legitimate authority ordained by God and not an imposter with self-serving motives.

The Credibility of the Vision

In addition, you must also be convicted about *what* you are serving, namely, the nature of the vision or the cause that you are committing yourself to, and you must be assured that it is God-inspired and not a fabrication of your leadership's imagination, and that this is for a wider global purpose rather than for the leader's selfish gain.

The Aligning of Self

Once convicted and assured of the *who* and the *what,* you must align yourself accordingly to that leadership and vision.

The Submitting of Self

Together with the aligning comes the submission to that leadership and vision.

Seeing the Future Greatness of Your Leadership

As a wise servant, you will discern and see the future greatness of the leadership you are serving even though the circumstances show otherwise. That way, you do not despise the days of small beginnings or miss out on your hour of visitation (namely, your future greatness).

The Respecting of the Anointing

Finally, as a discerning servant, you will understand that by recognizing, accepting and respecting the anointing, grace and gifting upon the leadership you are serving, you automatically become a partaker and a beneficiary of the same qualities that reside on and in your leader because you can never benefit or partake of anything that you do not recognize, accept and respect.

The strategy in Servanthood

By dealing with all the above elements, you will then advance beyond *who* and *what* to *how* all these aspects work together in you towards effective servanthood. In other words, you will grow in your understanding of what your purpose is in serving.

6. A ROOTING

This involves a strategic locating of the place and sphere where you have been ordained and called to serve.

"Get the right people on the bus in the right seats." **(Jim Collins)**

Therefore, we also, since we are surrounded by so great a cloud of witnesses, let us lay aside every weight, and the sin which so easily ensnares us, and let us run with endurance the race that is set before us. **(Hebrews 12:1)**

Running the right race in the right lane

Beyond discovering that you have a call to serve, beyond defining your identity and being secure in it, beyond making a decision to embark on that call, beyond dedicating to that call and beyond making a determined acknowledgment of the authority of the leadership, as a strategic servant you must then discern and locate your specific area of servanthood, because true servanthood entails not only running the right race but also running in the right lane.

Sitting in the right seat on the right bus

As an obedient servant, you will not only ensure you have boarded the "vision bus" that your leadership has been ordained to drive, you should also ensure that you are sitting in the right seat. Your leader's vision bus has other servants too, and each has their allotted place.

Finding the right position in the right place

As a dutiful servant, you must also ascertain your specific position, post and assignment within the vision bus, the one for which you have been equipped and endowed.

Grace for your Place

Your place/position is where you will thrive and experience a supernatural grace to operate, but at the same time it will be where you face your greatest battles and obstacles.

"Run your own race and stay in your own lane. God has a specific path for you where you will excel." **(Buky Oje Labi)**

Where You are Celebrated not Tolerated

Suffice to say that your place of assignment and purpose is where you will be celebrated not tolerated. It is where you will exert positive impact, influence and transformational change and where you will be received and accepted as one who belongs there.

Positioning and aligning

As a wise servant, you will locate and position yourself at your place of purpose logistically, aligning yourself strategically to your leadership and the vision.

A voice in your place

You must understand that you were born and are equipped and endowed for a specific place and sphere in your society and nation where you must become a voice.

7. A RELINQUISHING

This refers to a dying to self through the process of being developed as a servant.

"When Jesus calls a man, he bids him come and die" **(Dietrich Bonhoeffer).**

"None of us is there yet, but if we each have this attitude, we will put to death our reactions to criticisms and offenses. And though we may still stumble, we will learn that carrying the cross is not merely dying to self; it is embracing the love of Christ that forgives the very ones who have crucified us, that the battle that comes against us has actually driven us into the embrace of God." **(Francis Frangipane)**

I have been crucified with Christ; it is no longer I who live, but Christ lives in me; and the life which I now live in the flesh I live by faith in the Son of God, who loved me and gave Himself for me. **(Galatians 2:20)**

A voluntary dying

Beyond discovering that you have a call to serve, beyond defining your identity, beyond making a decision to embark on that call, beyond dedicating to that call, beyond making a determined acknowledgment of the authority of the leadership, and discerning and locating your specific area of servanthood, as a servant you should die to self.

Dying through a process

Servanthood is not born, but developed over time through a process of pruning, purging, threshing and the moulding of a person's character, attitude and mind-set designed to bring forth the qualities and characteristics of a true servant. Dying to self will come as a result of having undergone severe trials and tests, wilderness experiences and fiery furnaces, that will remove anything in you that could hinder your servanthood, while at the same time building in you the right foundation and fortitude for true servanthood.

Dying to what is fleshly and carnal

As a true servant, you must undergo a process of formation which will entail a dying to self, a dying to carnal and freshly desires and worldly appetites and wants, as well as dying to greed, materialism and all forms of lust.

"Dying to self means that self is no longer the reason for one's existence." (**Dr. D. W Eksternd**)

Dying to self-centeredness

This process of formation will cause you to die to all self-interests, self-absorption, self-focus, self-centeredness, selfish agendas and selfish ambitions.

"Sin is man's determination to manage by himself" (**Rudolf Bultmann**).

When we die to self, we dethrone the ego and empty our lives of self-serving priorities.

Put off, concerning your former conduct, the old man which grows corrupt according to the deceitful lusts and be renewed in the spirit of your mind. (**Ephesians 4:22-23**)

Dying to being self-oriented

By its very nature, true servanthood must be devoid of self because it entails being sacrificial and selfless, focusing on others, serving the interests of another and not one's own.

Dying to wrong attitudes

Dying to wrong attitudes and desires will produce a character with right attitudes and right passions.

*Then Jesus said to them all, "If anyone desires to come after Me, let him deny himself, and take up his cross daily, and follow Me." (**Luke 9:23**)*

Dying through radical surgery

Dying to self will require invasive surgery in areas such as your mind-set, your perception/vision, hearing, speech, heart condition, work ethics, handling of power, dreams and visions, your prayer life, your walk and your lifestyle.

*Therefore, we were buried with Him through baptism into death, that just as Christ was raised from the dead by the glory of the Father, even so we also should walk in newness of life. (**Romans 6:4**)*

Thought-Provoking Questions for Discussion

1. Do you feel you have discovered your own purpose? How did you discover it?

2. Do you feel you have come to a place where you know who you are in terms of your identity? If so, what things define you and what things do not?

3. About what kinds of issues have you had to make an irrevocable decision? Did you stick to that decision and, if so, what helped you to do that? If not, what caused you not to? Do you feel you have made an irrevocable decision concerning your call and purpose?

4. What factors normally hinder you from resolving to commit and dedicate yourself to your purpose and calling?

5. What authority figures are there currently in your life? How did you determine that they were your leaders? Have you ever struggled with the legitimacy of an authority figure and, if so, how did you deal with it?

6. Have you yet distinguished and located your sphere, place and position of assignment? If so, what road signs guided you on the way? If not, what difficulties are you encountering in locating your place?

7. What issues and habits in your life point to the fact that you have not yet died to self? What really hinders you from totally dying to self?

THE 7 ESSENTIAL ELEMENTS OF SERVANTHOOD

Opening Remarks

There are seven essential elements to functioning and effective servanthood. These include the following: (1) entering a consensual covenant, (2) believing in a vibrant vision, (3) forging a concrete connection, (4) sharing a common goal, (5) holding your leadership in high honour and respect, (6) observing a sacred stewardship, and (7) understanding and implementing the intricate measure of relating between the leadership you're called to serve and you, the servant. In this matter, the one serving must discern when to take up a position. This will largely depend on seasons and circumstances during your servanthood. Being wrongly positioned can greatly prejudice the leadership you serve and be extremely detrimental to your leadership's vision. As regards positioning, then, you must be sensitive, alert and logistical.

A servant's ability to discern the purpose and power of each position is critical to the welfare of their leadership and the vision. A true servant must master the precise art of positioning. A wise servant will be strategically aligned to their leadership in every aspect of life, just so long as this can be achieved practically and without breaching the boundaries of propriety. Alignment in this context refers to giving support to a person or a cause because you agree with what that person or cause represents. Such strategic alignment means physical, mental and emotional support.

The 7 Sevens

1. A CONSENSUAL COVENANT

"If one accepts the terms of the covenant and obeys God's law, he or she receives the blessings associated with the covenant." **(Russell M. Nelson)**

Can two walk together, unless they are agreed? Amos 3:3

A divine covenant

A covenant, whether written or not, is a solemn pledge, promise or pact between two or more people. True servanthood is usually founded on a covenant between three parties – God, the person doing the serving and the leadership. Serving is therefore a divine covenant. The covenant between the servant and their leadership is divine because it incorporates God as a party to the covenant in accordance with kingdom principles.

"A covenant made with God should be regarded not as restrictive but as protective" **(Russell M. Nelson).**

A covenant to serve God

The leadership has a mandate and a vision from God, so they are serving God and God's vision, while the servant has a call to serve the leadership as the leadership serves the Lord.

Ultimately, the servant is serving God through their leadership.

"There's nothing better than following and serving a leadership that's following and serving God." **(Anonymous)**

A covenant with obligations

A covenant does not signify a relationship in general, as is commonly assumed today. Rather, a covenant refers to a specific type of relationship. One of the fundamental elements of a covenant is that it imposes specific obligations on each party to perform and fulfil. It is a bilateral acceptance of obligations which are consensually agreed, not imposed.

A covenant with benefits

Another fundamental element of a covenant is that it will contain benefits for those who perform and fulfil their respective obligations. A covenant is relational because it always involves two parties. It is specifically a relationship of obligation because it binds one or both of the parties to certain specified duties.

Two are better than one, because they have a good reward for their labour. (**Ecclesiastes 4:9**)

A breach of covenant prejudices servanthood

In this relationship between the leadership and the servant, failure by either party to perform their specific obligations will seriously prejudice the vision.

"If we will keep our covenants, our covenants will keep us spiritually safe" (**Elder Neal Maxwell**).

A covenant is binding in nature

The validity of a covenant lies in its binding effect. A covenant can also create a new relationship like the covenant between Joshua and the Gibeonites (Joshua 9:15–20). They created a new relationship of peace where previously there had been enmity. A covenant is established because it is entered by choice rather than by necessity, and it is thereby binding upon both parties.

A covenant leads to commitment

The sealing of a leadership-servant relationship with a covenant guarantees long-term loyalty and deep commitment. A covenant does not initiate a relationship; rather, what a covenant does is formalize and give concrete expression to an arrangement which is already in existence. In other words, it gives backing to a pre-existing arrangement and adds solemnity to this agreement.

A Cautious Caveat

Notwithstanding the above, any covenant you align yourself to in this regard must of course not contravene the Word of God, the law of the land, nor your personal values. Even thieves and murderers have covenants which are binding! The unspoken maxim, "Honour among thieves," is a covenant of sorts.

2. A TESTED TRUST

"Trusting is hard; knowing who to trust is even harder." (**Maria V Snyder**)

Trust is interdependent

A leadership-servant relationship involves a deep trust and interdependence between the two parties. The leadership must be able to rely on the servant fully, without any fear of betrayal. Likewise, the servant must be able to trust in the vision and agenda of the leadership. The trust between a servant and their leadership will inevitably be tested by various factors but it must stand the test of time.

"Trust starts with truth and ends with truth." (**Santosh Kalwar**)

Trust is sacred

True servanthood is founded on a tested trust between the leadership and the servant, whereby there is a deep unspoken and sacred trust in each other. Sacred means that it is extremely precious, valuable and to be respected.

Trust is crucial for servanthood

Without the servant having trust in the leadership and the vision, they cannot serve effectively and confidently. Without a leader trusting their servant, they cannot instruct them or rely on them effectively because they will consciously or subconsciously be guarding against betrayal and breaches of confidentiality.

"Trust is the glue of life. It is the foundational principle that holds relationships together." (**Stephen Covey**)

Trust is granted and earned

A servant's responsibility towards their leadership is to maintain strict confidentiality with regards to all matters pertaining to their leadership, in order to earn trust from their leadership.

Exhort bondservants to be obedient to their own masters, to be well pleasing in all things, not answering back, not pilfering, but showing all good fidelity, that they may adorn the doctrine of God our Saviour in all things. (**Titus 2:9-10**)

Breach of trust is costly

A breach of trust by a servant exposes a leader to dangers, especially from their enemies.

Trust allows vulnerability

When a leader has complete trust in their servant, they can be vulnerable and open in sharing their deepest thoughts and fears, knowing that they are safe and secure.

"Trust is built when someone is vulnerable and not taken advantage of" (**Bob Vanourek**).

Trust is built over time

A true servant will have been tested over a long period of time before they can be trusted by their leader. A good servant will guard against breaching their leadership's trust. While it takes a long time to build trust, it takes a minute to break and destroy that trust. It then takes a long time to rebuild the trust again.

"For there to be betrayal, there has to have been trust first." (**Suzanne Collins**)

The above notwithstanding, trust must be a two-way traffic so that you must also trust your leadership as much as they trust you. There are many sad cases where a leader truly trusts their servant because they know that this servant will die for them. However, the leader may not be as eager even to give a small measure of assistance to their servant during a tough personal situation or crisis, let alone die for them. Some leaders will throw their servants under the bus when under pressure. In other cases, servants have gone to jail because their leaders betrayed the trust between them, maybe by blackmailing a servant, or vice versa, using information entrusted to the other.

3. A VIBRANT VISION

"The only thing worse than being blind is having sight but no vision." (**Hellen Keller**)

Where there is no revelation, the people cast off restraint. (**Proverbs 29:18**)

An authentic vision

True servanthood is founded on there being a vision which the leader believes they have received from God. Whenever you begin to doubt your leader's vision is genuine, you cannot serve effectively. You must persist in believing that your leader's vision is from God.

A vision is a roadmap

A vision is a roadmap enabling you to create transformative initiatives that bring benefit to targeted groups that are on the up-and-up.

A vision evolves with time

As a servant, you must realize that the vision will continue to grow, so you must also be ready to grow in order to be effective.

A true vision is global

Both the leader and the servant must be aware that the vision is intended to impact millions of people. This is the reason both parties guard it jealously and ensure they fulfil it.

A vision that draws and pulls

The vision must be vibrant and compelling if it is to draw more supporters; the bigger the vision, the more likely it is that leaders and servants cannot cope on their own.

A vision that retains its DNA

The vision must remain pure and defiled and on course, not becoming distorted or deviating from its original purpose.

A vision that is bigger than the bearer

The vision must be bigger than the leadership and the servant and it must transcend personal limitations. The vision must remain in its original form. Though it may evolve and expand positively, it must fundamentally retain the original intention and its original DNA. If this fails to happen, you are free to walk away from serving that vision, if attempts to point out the problem to the leadership have fallen on deaf ears. It is also better to leave instead of remaining while criticizing the leader. In a non-profit organization, for example, a leader may begin using donated funds for their own benefits, leaving the intended beneficiaries destitute. To that extent, the vision has become distorted and lost its original purpose.

4. A CONCRETE CONNECTION

A knitted bond

There is a strong bond between leaders and servants. If the vision they are both serving is to progress, there must be a joining and knitting of their hearts, minds and souls.

An alignment of two into one

This concrete connection between a servant and their leader will entail both being mentally, emotionally and spiritually aligned in order to effectively fulfil the vision.

And a certain centurion's servant, who was dear to him, was sick and ready to die. **(Luke 7:2)**

The centurion's servant was dear to him; they had a connection. This was what bound them together as leader and servant.

A united front

This connection is based on a united front so that each can fulfil a call and purpose, knowing that united they stand, but divided they fall.

Guarding against disconnection

A sensitive servant and leadership will discern when the connection between them loosens, either out of a broken trust or because of attacks by internal or external forces, such as people who seek to separate them in order to prejudice the vision.

"There are no bonds so strong as those which are formed by suffering together" **(Harriet Ann Jacobs).**

Enemies of your connection

It is therefore the responsibility of a faithful servant to guard against anything that could interfere negatively with this concrete connection. You do this by refusing to entertain any negative feedback about your leader, and by not associating with people who are known enemies of your leader. These people may seek to defile this connection between you in order to torpedo the vision.

Your connection exudes public confidence

This concrete connection between a servant and their leader is of vital importance for the targeted beneficiaries of the vision and for the supporters of the vision. When these invested parties see a united front between the leader and their servant, it gives them the confidence to trust in the vision.

Your connection is empowering

A faithful servant must continuously maintain this concrete connection because it is on this connection that a large percentage of their ability to serve is based. There is an anointing and an empowerment that flows from a leader to a servant, enabling the servant to perform beyond their usual ability and capacity.

A CAUTIOUS CAVEAT

This connection, which is usually emotional, mental and spiritual, should not go beyond the vision into, for example, asexual connection or a destructive soul tie. The connection must remain pure, decent and moral, fit for its intended purpose. It is not uncommon for a wicked leader to manipulate and confuse a faithful servant into believing that their concrete connection must extend to sexual and soulish ties. You must guard against this.

5. A COMMON GOAL

"We all have a common goal, and we know it's all for our future good." **(Marta Kristen)**

United in their definition of a greater goal

A servant and their leadership must agree what they mean by a greater goal. The goal is usually global in outreach, public in nature and universal in its application.

"I like the common goal initiative, the vision as a tool for social change and the power to improve the world." **(Juan Mata)**

United in the definition of what is a greater good

A servant and their leader must agree what they mean by a greater good- that it positively impacts people, empowers them and advances their welfare.

"If you don't live a life of servanthood of a greater good, you've got to at least die a death in servanthood of a greater good." **(John Green)**

United in their execution of the greater goal

This means that a servant and their leader must agree on the methodology and the pace of implementing the greater goal.

"Through common goals, we are creating a collaborative way to give back to society." **(Juan Mata)**

United in their levels of passion

A servant and their leader will both be passionate about fulfilling the greater goal.

United in setting aside their personal interests and agendas

A servant and their leader will put the greater goal above their own individual goals and ensure that they do not allow a conflict between the greater goal and their own.

"It is a rare opportunity when you do something for the greater good." **(Scott Borchetta)**

United in remaining on track

A servant and their leadership do not allow a derailing of the greater goal or a distortion of its definition.

United in their understanding as to who is leading and who is following

Where a difference arises with any of the above, as a servant you must respectfully surrender and submit yourself to the direction of the leadership because the leadership is the one who is the vision bearer.

A Cautious Caveat

Even though the leader and the servant are united in the desired outcome, the methodology is critical. There must be some understanding, however it is communicated, that where the methods of fulfilling the vision go against the Word of God, the law of the land or accepted practice and traditions, then as a servant you are free to walk away. If the person you are serving chooses to go the wrong way, the end must never justify the means.

6. A HIGH HONOUR

"Honour is a gift you give freely." **(Craig Croeschel)**

Let as many bondservants as are under the yoke count their own masters worthy of all honour, so that the name of God and His doctrine may not be blasphemed. **(1 Timothy 6:1)**

Admiration and praise

As a servant, honouring your leaders will entail esteeming them because of the qualities you recognize in them that are admirable and praiseworthy.

Respect and esteem

Honouring will also entail respecting your leaders, holding them in high regard.

Value and treasure

You will treasure your leaders because you recognize that they are a rare gift that you and others need. You will also treasure the vision they are bearing because when you honour someone, you will value what they value.

Reverence and deference

There will be reverence and deference as well as polite submission when you are dealing with your leaders; this is a sign of honour.

Homage and allegiance

Honouring entails paying homage to your leaders, as well as pledging allegiance and loyalty to them.

Honour despite all

You honour and respect your leaders not because they are perfect but because weaknesses or failures on their part do not erode the respect due to them. As a mature servant, you will know the difference.

*Servants, be submissive to your masters with all fear, not only to the good and gentle, but also to the harsh. (**1 Peter 2:18**)*

To love is to honour

True respect and honour are founded on a sincere and pure love that a servant has for their leaders. It is difficult to serve, honour and respect what you do not love.

"Be honourable yourself if you wish to associate with honourable people." **(Proverb)**

A Cautious Caveat

True and sincere honour that is given to a leader is usually earned by that leader. It is difficult to honour one who has become dishonourable, because doing that will also make you dishonourable. You will also have lost respect for yourself by serving someone who has lost the right to be respected and honoured. While it is not your business to judge or deal with a dishonourable leader (that is God's mandate and the mandate of other legitimate human authorities), you can choose to walk away without speaking evil, scandalizing or defaming that leader.

7. A SACRED STEWARDSHIP

Stewardship is defined as the careful and responsible management of something entrusted to one's care.

"A time is coming when each of us will have to give account of our stewardship" **(Sunday Adelaja).**

For to everyone who has, more will be given, and he will have abundance; but from him who does not have, even what he has will be taken away. **(Matthew 13:12)**

Defining stewardship

A steward is someone entrusted with another's wealth or property and charged with the responsibility of managing it in the owner's best interests.

Your leader's life

True servanthood will entail you being entrusted with your leader's life. You must therefore guard and manage it fiercely and jealously. This requires you protecting the integrity of the vision against being hijacked, derailed or distorted.

Your leader's reputation

A sacred stewardship requires a servant to manage and guard their leader's reputation from slander and defamation because a good reputation is an invaluable asset.

Your leader's welfare

This also requires managing the expectations of the beneficiaries of the vision by representing your leader correctly to them, thereby guarding the leader's welfare.

Your leader's relationships

Stewardship in general includes managing/guarding the relationships between your leader and their supporters and benefactors.

Your leader's resources

You must steward your leader's resources and their vision prudently (Genesis 39:5-6).

Your leader's documents and information

This part of stewardship is sacred because it also requires managing and guarding confidential documents and information belonging to the leader and relating to the vision.

"Stewardship is the use of God-given resources for the accomplishment of God-given goals" **(Ron Blue)**.

A Cautious Caveat

Your ability to be a good steward of your leader's resources and vision largely depends on your leader's ability to be a good steward. Without that, your attempts at good stewardship may constantly be thwarted by the negligence and carelessness of the leader. An example might be a political leader who may constantly break the government's rules regarding the use of official motor vehicles, thereby making it impossible for you to be effective in your stewardship. When poor stewardship affects the welfare of the organization, government and nation, and then translates to the poor welfare of the people, you may make the decision to expose and disclose the matter to higher authorities.

His lord said to him, 'Well done, good and faithful servant; you have been faithful over a few things, I will make you ruler over many things. Enter into the joy of your lord.' **(Matthew 25:23)**

Thought Provoking Questions for Discussion

1. Have you ever entered a consensual covenant and, if so, what was it about?

2. Have you ever broken a sacred trust or has someone ever broken your trust? How did it feel and what were the consequences?

3. Are you currently serving another person's vision? How did you know you had been called to serve that vision? Do you have a vision of your own?

4. Have you ever been in a concrete connection with anyone? What factors cemented that concrete connection and what challenges threatened it?

5. Do you have a common cause with anyone or any group of persons? How did you identify and locate one another?

6. What factors may affect or have affected your ability to have a high honour and regard for an authority figure you are serving, or have served in the past?

7. Have you ever been entrusted with a sacred stewardship? What challenges and temptations, if any, did you encounter?

THE 7 CONSCIOUS CHOICES IN THE WORD S.E.R.V.A.N.T

"The power of choice is one of the greatest gifts bestowed upon man." **(Anonymous)**

The word S.E.R.V.A.N.T. spells and speaks to some conscious choices you will need to make to seal your servanthood. These choices are to serve sacrificially, to listen emphatically, to serve with revelation, to be fully vested in your servanthood, to remain nameless as you serve, to pledge allegiance continuously as you serve, and finally to remain true to your servanthood, in and out of season.

The 7 Sevens

1. TO SERVE SACRIFICIALLY

I beseech you therefore, brethren, by the mercies of God, that you present your bodies a living sacrifice, holy, acceptable to God, which is your reasonable service. **(Romans 12:1)**

Servanthood is Sacrifice

Sacrificial servanthood defines a servanthood that goes beyond the call of duty, often putting aside things beneficial to oneself.

"For a sacrifice to be real, it must cost, it must hurt, and it must lead to a complete emptying of ourselves." **(Mother Teresa)**

Sacrifice entails passion

Serving sacrificially demonstrates deep passion to the call.

Sacrifice entails deep commitment

It also demonstrates a deep commitment to the cause.

Sacrifice is an act of love

It demonstrates a sincere love for the one you are serving. As Jesus said, "Even the Son of Man did not come to be served but to serve and to give his life a ransom for many" (Mark 10:45).

Sacrifice leads to successful outcomes

It also demonstrates a genuine desire for successful outcomes through the accomplishment of set goals.

Sacrifice may entail pain and suffering

Serving sacrificially will entail pain and endurance through hardships and sufferings, going through fiery furnaces until you die to selfish indulgences and comforts.

Sacrifice may entail incurring losses

Serving sacrificially may often mean that you will suffer some losses in one way or another - the loss of leisure time and friendships, for instance - but these you will be compensated and rewarded for in the long-term.

A Cautious Caveat

It is important to qualify what it means to serve your leader sacrificially. Sacrifice must be in line with your other responsibilities, such as family, and your other obligations for service in other sectors. God is not a God of confusion and he will give you wisdom to balance everything in terms of resources, time and energy. Failure to have a balance will bring sorrow. A case in point is where a committed woman ends up giving her wealth to a leader and their vision, thereby leaving her family destitute and desperate. Another would be where a secretary or a personal assistant ends up offering her leader very inappropriate services in the guise of sacrificial servanthood, thereby not only breaching proper boundaries but also leading her to offer herself beyond reasonable hours of work.

2. TO LISTEN EMPATHETICALLY

"Empathy is seeing with the eyes of another, listening with the ears of another, and feeling with the heart of another." (**Anonymous**)

A wise man will hear and increase learning, and a man of understanding will attain wise counsel. (**Proverbs 1:5**)

So then, my beloved brethren, let every man be swift to hear, slow to speak, slow to wrath. (**James 1:19**)

He who has ears to hear, let him hear! (**Matthew 11:15**)

The art of listening

The art of listening is crucial in servanthood because the very nature of serving requires you to take and implement instructions from another.

Seeking first to understand before being understood

Empathetic listening is seeking first to understand the other person before seeking to be understood. The opposite is when a servant 'listens' with an agenda to reply. In this scenario, even while a leader is still giving instructions, the servant's mind is busy preparing their response, meaning that they are not really paying attention.

"Wisdom is the reward you get for a lifetime of listening when you would have preferred to talk" (**Doug Larson**).

Active listening

This involves taking time to actively listen without getting distracted, defocused or derailed - paying attention and giving the speaker your undivided attention.

"You cannot truly listen to anyone and do anything else at the same time." (**M. Scott Peck**)

Offering empathy

Empathetic listening is offering empathy instead of sympathy. The difference between empathy and sympathy is that empathy is the ability to experience the feeling of the other person, while sympathy is being able to vocalise the suffering of the other person. Empathy is putting yourself in another person's shoes and therefore requires a higher level of listening.

Listening with the right body language

Empathetic listening is paying attention to your body language, posture and tone of voice to ensure that you are genuinely and emotionally engaged with the person who is taking the time and trust to share with you.

"Empathy is seeing the eyes of another, listening with the ears of another, and feeling with the heart of another" (**Anonymous**).

Quick to listen but slow to speak

Empathetic listening means refraining from offering solutions prematurely or hastily, and first waiting to really understand the issues at hand.

"We think we listen, but very rarely do we listen with real understanding, true empathy. Yet listening, of this very special kind, is one of the most potent forces for change that I know" (**Carl Rodgers**).

Real listening requires trust

Empathetic listening enables a servant to gain the trust of the person to whom they are listening. A true servant must be an excellent listener in order to be an excellent implementer and executor of instructions.

A Cautious Caveat

You must of course qualify and guard what you listen to because empathetic listening is only healthy and wholesome where what is being said and the instructions being given are also healthy and wholesome. This means that the content of what you are listening to must be legal, moral and ethical.

3. TO SERVE WITH REVELATION

What revelation is and what it is not

Revelation refers to the insight and understanding of something, to arriving at a knowledge of something. Serving with revelation means not serving with misconception or presumption. The opposite of serving by revelation is serving carnally which cannot last because the flesh will eventually get weary and abort the life of servanthood.

A revelation is deeply personal and often difficult to explain to another person, or difficult for another person to understand. A true servant should avoid trying to justify or explain themselves to others who have no real revelation of servanthood. The servant receives personal revelation in the following areas:

*Revelation as to the **who***

As a servant, you will receive revelation concerning *who* you are serving – namely, the nature, character and temperament of your leader.

*Revelation as to the **what***

As a servant, you will also gain revelation about *what* you are serving – namely, the vision or cause. This may involve understanding the dynamics of that vision and owning it.

*Revelation as to the **why***

You will also receive revelation about *why* you are serving your leader and their vision by understanding the intended goals, objectives and benefits.

*Revelation as to the **where***

You will also receive revelation *where* you are to serve - meaning your place and position within the leader's life and vision.

*Revelation as to the **how***

You will also receive revelation as to *how* you are to serve in terms of your roles and responsibilities.

Revelation as to what   motivates servanthood

You will also receive a revelation that true servanthood is motivated by love and not fear, that your true fulfilment and greatness comes from serving and not being served.

A Cautious Caveat

Revelation regarding servanthood must of course be within the confines and limits of God and the law of the land. You cannot purport to say that you have a revelation about servanthood to which nobody else seems to bear witness, and which fails to align with the Word of God and the law of the land. Remember 2 Peter 1:20:

"Knowing this first, that no prophecy of Scripture is of any private interpretation."

Many cults are born out of exclusive personalized revelations which have not been subjected to any scrutiny or vetting. It is not uncommon for many well-meaning people to end up in cults because they have followed unfounded and baseless revelations. Even in the corporate sector, it is not unheard of for one serving another to include sexual favours based on some personalized revelation that he/she has.

4. TO BE VESTED IN YOUR SERVANTHOOD

Sold out

This means totally committed to serving the leader and their vision.

Vested physically

That is, committed with your physical energy.

Vested emotionally

This means being committed in your heart by owning the vision, bearing the burdens of the leader and the vision by virtue of having owned the vision.

Vested mentally

This means being intellectually committed by ensuring that your mind-set and thoughts align with the best interests of the leader and the vision.

Vested spiritually

This means being spiritually vested so that you take time to speak the Word of God over the leader and the vision, interceding and praying for the success of the cause.

Vested long-term

This means being committed for the long run, not just for a season - fully committed in and out of season and in all seasons until the vision is successfully completed.

Owning the vision and being one with your leadership

Being vested means that, as a faithful servant, you become almost one with your leader and the vision.

A Cautious Caveat

You must keep in mind that there are other important aspects of your life that also require your investment. Vesting in servanthood must therefore be in proportion. Many careers and businesses have suffered and remained stagnant because someone chose to be completely sold out in serving a corporate organization, family enterprise or even a church vision, only to regret this years later. The vesting must be within the divine order of things because our God is not a God of confusion and He expects you to balance all aspects of your life.

5. TO PLEDGE ALLEGIANCE

No servant can serve two masters; for either he will hate the one and love the other, or else he will be loyal to the one and despise the other. You cannot serve God and mammon. **Luke 16:13**

Allegiance through words and actions

A true servant's allegiance is evidenced by what they do and say.

Allegiance must be seen and felt

A leader must be able to witness and experience the loyalty of their servant.

Allegiance must be reassured constantly

It is important for a servant to keep reinforcing their faithfulness, obedience to instructions, devotion to their mission and fidelity to the trust extended to them.

Allegiance is a solemn promise

To pledge allegiance is to make a solemn promise to be committed and loyal to one's leader and their vision.

Allegiance is devotion

It is an expression of devotion in the highest form of the word. Remember Joshua 24:24: *And the people said to Joshua, "The Lord our God we will serve, and His voice we will obey!"*

Allegiance is an oath

Allegiance often entails taking an oath, meaning to give your word as your bond, or as a guarantee, whether verbal or written.

Allegiance is a free choice

Allegiance can also entail a vow which is a form of covenant to serve and follow a leader. A pledge, oath or vow symbolizes the seriousness of the servant and is a free choice.

A Cautious Caveat

Your allegiance to your leader must align with your core values and principles. This means that while you may have pledged allegiance, if the person you are serving radically changes course and distorts the fundamentals of the original vision, if they also contradict the core of who you are, God's Word or the law of the land, you are justified in changing your allegiance. Many faithful people serving in the corporate sector, or in various departments of government, may find their careers in jeopardy because of blindly pledging allegiance to an over-zealous CEO or a County Governor who is no longer on the right path. Your allegiance therefore must be assessed continuously in line with what you agreed originally.

6. TO SERVE AND REMAIN NAMELESS

"Further, take heed that you faithfully perform the business you have to do in the world, from a regard to the commands of God; and not from an ambitious desire of being esteemed better than others." **(David Brainerd)**

Very truly I tell you, no servant is greater than his master, nor is a messenger greater than the one who sent him. (John 13:16)

Maintaining a low profile

As a true servant, you will take a low profile by not seeking to be seen or take the limelight from your leader. In John 13:1-5, Jesus washed the disciples' feet, but this did not dent his sense of identity. Likewise, as a servant, you must remain secure in your identity which means knowing who you are and God's promises and plans for you.

Servanthood without drama

You serve behind the scenes without drama and fanfare or drawing attention to yourself.

Servanthood without accolades

You are to serve without seeking praise, tirelessly and sometimes without being thanked.

Not so with you. Instead, whoever wants to become great among you must be your servant, and whoever wants to be first must be your servant. (Matthew 20:26)

Private servanthood matches public servanthood

This means serving as excellently in private as you would serve in public. Whatever you do in private by way of service, one day you will be publicly acknowledged and rewarded for this. You do not just serve well when you are being seen.

Letting your leader shine

A servant who humbly serves behind the scenes, allows their leadership to shine, to take credit for victories and successes.

No competitive spirit

A servant with a competitive spirit will seek accolades and recognition. If they do not receive these, they will easily abandon their servanthood.

No public recognition

A servant seeking to sabotage or undermine their leader will seek to show that they did all the work. You must remember that titles and positions do not define your identity, your calling and purpose do. In short, your servanthood should not threaten your identity.

It is very revealing that we never get to know the name of Jonathan's armour-bearer even though he is one of the best examples of a true servant, one who was with his master heart and soul.

A Cautious Caveat

Your namelessness is of course in the context of ensuring that you do not seek to undermine the leader you are serving. You must not be consumed with the promotion of your own name. In promoting the name and vision of your leader, you do not lose your identity, fall into total oblivion, lose your self-esteem and confidence. Rather, you must remember who you are even as you serve. Your identity is in Christ. This is where your relevance and value are found. Some people who have served faithfully have sadly lost all sense of identity so that even when the opportunity arises and God begins to reward them and promote them, they become reluctant to shine because they have long forgotten who they were. Remaining nameless as you serve, suspending your own vision, does not mean losing your identity or killing your own vision and destiny.

7. TO SERVE BY REMAINING TRUE

Let your 'Yes' be 'Yes,' and your 'No,' 'No.' For whatever is more than these is from the evil one. (**Matthew 5:37**)

The integrity of the upright will guide them, but the perversity of the unfaithful will destroy them. (**Proverbs 11:3**)

True in and out of season

During your servanthood, you will undergo various seasons where you will experience severe testing, trials and tribulations You will need to evade the many traps and potholes on the way. Being human, you may be tempted to lose focus, loyalty and commitment but you must be strong and remain true in and out of season irrespective of all the hardships.

Remaining true is a choice

A faithful servant will make a conscious choice to remain true in and out of season and unconditionally.

Remaining true is a heart attitude

Remaining true entails embracing the right attitudes, right heart conditions, roles and responsibilities of your servanthood, doing these things faithfully, no matter what.

We are taking pains to do what is right, not only in the eyes of the Lord but also in the eyes of man. (**2 Corinthians 8:2**)

Remaining true is costly

The choice to remain true means the servant may suffer persecution from those seeking to derail them.

Remaining true means preventing sabotage

As a true servant, you will encounter the equivalent of Tobias and Sanballat, people who seek to tempt you away from your servanthood and to sabotage your call (Nehemiah 4:3).

Offence hinders remaining true

As a faithful servant, beware of becoming offended or resentful towards your leader. Betrayal is the opposite of remaining true.

Remaining true is action beyond words

Remaining true is not paying lip service; it is demonstrated by right actions because actions speak louder than words.

A Cautious Caveat

Your ability to remain true and authentic will be based on the leader also remaining true and authentic. You cannot serve someone or something whose authenticity and truth have been eroded. To do that will make you hypocritical. When you lose your authenticity, you lose your effectiveness in servanthood.

"You are only effective when you are authentic." (**T. D. Jakes**)

A case in point: a young campaign manager was serving an aspiring candidate for the office of governor. A time came when he was no longer able to remain true to his leader; he was constantly unable to agree with policies and instructions which were totally illegal and ungodly. The young man says that instead of quitting, he continued to pretend that he agreed with what was going on, which led him down a very dark path which he regrets. Continuing to serve a leader who has lost his way and is doing things you do not agree with will, at the very least, turn you into a very dishonest and immoral person, and at the very worst land you in jail. It is better to quit than pretend to be true to what you know is not.

Thought Provoking Questions for Discussion

1. What sacrifices do you feel you have made and what losses have you incurred during your servanthood?

2. What factors hinder you from listening empathetically and how have you sought to improve your empathetic listening?

3. Have you encountered people - even those close to you - who did not understand your call to serve? Do you feel you have understood the five revelations of servanthood– namely, the *who* you are serving, the *what* you are serving, the *why* you are serving, the *where* you should serve and the *how* you should serve?

4. Do you feel that you are totally and fully vested in your servanthood? If not, what hinders you? What do you feel you have vested in your servanthood?

5. What frustrations have you encountered, if any, in having to remain nameless in your servanthood? What temptations did you have to overcome in wanting to be known and be given credit as you served?

6. Have you ever felt uncomfortable about giving allegiance to those you are serving and, if so, what made you uncomfortable and how did you deal with it?

7. Do you feel that you have remained true and authentic in your servanthood and if not, what interfered with that and how did you deal with it?

Chapter 2

YOUR PERSONA AS A SERVANT

Defining Your Self-Identity As You Serve

"I am Thy servant to do Thy will, and that will is sweeter to me than position or riches or fame, and I choose it above all things on earth or in heaven." ~ (A. W. Tozer)

Chapter Preview

The 7 Characteristics of a True Servant

1. Loyalty
2. Submissiveness
3. Selflessness
4. Commitment
5. Obedience
6. Trustworthiness
7. Consistency

The 7 Hearts of a True Servant

1. An Open-Receptive Heart
2. A Pure Heart
3. A Brave Heart
4. A Big Heart
5. A Warm Heart
6. An Undivided Heart
7. A Jovial Heart

The 7 Competencies of a True Servant

1. Skilled
2. Effectiveness
3. Resourceful
4. Valuable
5. Effective Communication
6. Art of Self-Discipline
7. Notable

INTRODUCTION

Who is a servant? A servant is, by definition, someone who takes and carries out the instructions and orders of another - someone who is a devoted follower and supporter, willing to wait on another as an attendant.

A servant is accordingly someone who is engaged in servanthood. Servanthood is understood as the action of helping or doing work for someone else. The servant is understood as a person who serves others, performs duties for that person, someone subject to the direction or control of another.

True servanthood goes beyond employment or contractual engagement because it entails a conscious choice to live for another or others and not to live for self. Someone who has suspended their own interests to serve the interests of another has made a decision that is moral and spiritual in nature, and indeed in consequence.

"Servanthood to others is what brings true happiness" (**Marie Osmond**).

The disposition of servanthood does not come naturally to many of us. Often it is a concept that many people despise because they perceive it as shameful, demeaning or as a sign of being beneath or less than, or being owned, controlled and dominated by another, as in enslavement and bondage, where the servant is totally dependent and serves because they are compelled to, not because they have made a choice. When we choose to serve, servanthood is a joy.

"I slept and dreamt that life was joy. I awoke and saw that life was servanthood. I acted and behold, servanthood was joy" (**Rabindranath Tagore**)

While the world may interpret servanthood in a negative way, in the Bible it is seen as a noble calling. In the world's eyes, servanthood is often despised because it is more natural for the human mind to want to be served and many interpret success as synonymous with that. In the Bible, it is much better to serve than to be served.

A true servant will enter their sonship in Christ and then embrace a life of servanthood out of gratitude. Embracing servanthood without sonship will cause a person to feel like a slave. Entering sonship without embracing servanthood will cause a person to feel entitled.

"As we lose ourselves in the servanthood of others, we discover our own lives and our own happiness" **(Dieter F. Uchtdorf)**

A true servant will essentially ask themselves five key questions:

1. **Who** are you serving (God, Principal, society, or nation)?
2. **Why** are you serving (your motivation, is it a call or a chore? Are you expecting rewards from men or from God?)
3. **Where** are you serving (your sphere or sector and position)?
4. **What** are you serving (is it a vision or a selfish agenda? What is your brief?)?
5. **How** are you serving (your attitude and approach, including your principles, values, and codes)?

All these questions are extensively addressed and answered in this book.

In this chapter we examine the fundamentals about the *persona* of the servant – namely, your characteristics, your heart condition, and your competencies. When it comes to character and competence, it should be noted that they make up the two prongs of a pair of scissors. No matter how impeccable your character is, you must also be competent for the task, and no matter how competent you are, you must also have the right character.

Sometimes the world looks for competence instead of character while the church looks for character instead of competence. The two must go together because you can be competent without being a person of character and you can be a person of character without having any competence.

THE 7 CHARACTERISTICS OF A TRUE SERVANT

Having understood the nature of servanthood and the principles upon which it is founded, we can now address another crucial issue, namely the *characteristics* of a true servant.

Character is made up of the mental and moral qualities distinctive to an individual. This includes a person's personality, nature, position, temper, and temperament. As a Greek philosopher once said, "Watch your thoughts, they lead to attitudes; watch your attitudes, they lead to words; watch your words, they lead to actions; watch your actions, they lead to habits; watch your habits, they lead to character; watch your character, it leads to your destiny." Character is what defines you. Your character is defined by what you do when you think no one else is looking.

A servant's character must be exemplary and above reproach. Their ability to perform and serve faithful will inevitably depend mostly on their character, among other qualities. However, character without competency is insufficient because being a good person does not necessarily make you a capable person. Competency without character is inadequate for true servanthood, which is why character and competence must exist hand in hand, balancing each other.

"People are often interested in one's talents, but God is interested in one's character" **(Rick Warren).**

The characteristics of true servanthood involve the qualities, features, hallmarks, traits, attributes, habits, and mannerisms that identify a person. However, it must be noted that no one is perfect and that your character will be developed and moulded as you serve. Failures and weaknesses here and there are not the end of the world and errors in moral judgement can always be redeemed if you are humble and teachable. The idea is to constantly feed your strengths and starve your weaknesses. You must know your weaknesses so that you can deal with them and manage them. Do not let them pull you down and do not overemphasize or magnify them. Your words must match your actions and your character should be shaped by your everyday actions, thoughts, words, and habits.

The Sevens

1. LOYALTY

"Nothing is nobler and more venerable than loyalty. Cherish loyalty." **(Cicero)**

He has shown you, O man what is good; and what does the Lord require of you but to do justly, to love mercy and to walk humbly with your God. **(Micah 6:8)**

Loyalty is a hallmark of servanthood

Loyalty is one of the hallmarks of a true servant. It is defined by you remaining faithful to something - your word, a promise, or a person. Loyalty is unconditional love for an individual or a cause. It involves remaining present in good times and bad, in plenty and in poverty, in successes and calamities. "Loyalty is about people who stay true to you behind your back" (anonymous). An example in the Bible can be seen in one premium servant - Jonathan's armour-bearer - who told his leader, "I am with you heart and soul" (I

Samuel 14:7). "Loyalty means nothing unless it has as at its heart the absolute principle of self-sacrifice" (Woodrow Wilson).

Loyalty is respect irrespective

Loyalty is a strong feeling of allegiance and devotion. It means respecting your leader because God has chosen them. The loyal servant is someone who sincerely believes in their leader and vision. Loyalty means respecting your leader even when they are wrong. For example, King David ordered his servant Goab to do a census of the people, which Goab knew was wrong, but at David's insistence, he obeyed and as we read later King David suffered the consequences (1 Chronicles 21).

The key here is to check whether obeying instructions that do not feel right will lead to serious harm, or a contravention of God's law, or the law of the land.

"Loyalty means I am down with you whether you are wrong or right, but I will tell you when you are wrong and help you get it right" (**Anonymous**).

Loyalty is clinging not kissing

A true servant is a clinger not a kisser. A clinger identifies the leader whom God has chosen for them to serve. They will follow that leader without wavering or hesitation. A kisser, on the other hand, is one who will only follow if the season is positive and the conditions are conducive. They will not be in it for long haul.

"A man without loyalty will leave you once the road darkens" (**J. R. R. Tolkien**).

In the Bible, Shimei who chose to kiss instead of cling. He deserted and abandoned King David when the going got tough *(2 Samuel 16:5-13)*. In marked contrast, Ruth chose to cling to Naomi when they reached a crossroad (Ruth 1:16). It is interesting that Orpah, in a similar situation to Ruth's, chose to kiss Naomi goodbye instead of clinging to her.

Emotional deposits lead to loyalty

Loyalty means keeping your emotional bank account in credit, making sure that there are more deposits than withdrawals. The biggest proof that you are making deposits of loyalty is the fact that you are giving time to another because time is your most valuable resource.

Emotional withdrawals lead to disloyalty

The biggest withdrawal from your bank account, the greatest evidence of disloyalty, is when you break promises and fail to keep commitments to other people. This shows disrespect and is a sign that you are devaluing the other person.

"Loyalty is a 24/7 proposition. It's not a part-time job" (**Jonathan Moyo**).

Loyalty means balancing conflicting loyalties well

It is crucial that you come to discern when and where conflicting loyalties arise so that you learn to manage them and prioritize wisely without necessarily being disloyal to anyone of them. You will need to develop an ethical code when facing conflict between loyalties, e.g., loyalties to your spouse, family, leaders etc.

Loyalty must align to what is godly and ethical

You will also need to use God's Word and its principles in handling conflicting loyalties. Recognizing unreasonable demands from your leader is crucial, so that you can address them wisely and respectfully. You should not be loyal to a leader or a cause that distracts you from what really matters. Your moral code must be your compass. You must however respect your leader's title and position even if you cannot respect the person.

A Cautious Caveat

Notwithstanding the above, you cannot be loyal unconditionally without vetting what you are being loyal to, especially if that loyalty leads to harming others and causing distraction. For example, Hitler's followers were loyal to him unconditionally to the point of participating in acts that were unspeakably evil and, without doubt, both contrary to the Word of God and indeed to international law. Your loyalty to your leader cannot go beyond your obedience to God, nor beyond the law of the land.

2. SUBMISSIVENESS

"Submission is not about authority; it is all about relationships of love and respect." (William Paul Young)

Obey those who rule over you, and be submissive, for they watch out for your souls, as those who must give account. Let them do so with joy and not with grief, for that would be unprofitable for you. **(Hebrews 13:17)**

Submission is foundational to servanthood

A leader-servant relationship cannot truly exist without submission. Submission is the action of accepting and yielding to the superior authority of another person. There are different types of authorities to whom one should submit but for our context here we will deal with the leader-servant relationship.

"Submission does not mean being weak or passive. It is the opposite because true power and strength reside in submission" (Elif Safak)

Submission is voluntary not coerced

True submission is voluntary and never forced; it stems from a free choice made in your heart. Any submission that is not freely given is not submission at all. A submitted servant knows their position vis-à-vis their leader and accepts that position voluntarily, and without resistance.

Submission arises from relationship

Submission at its best arises from a meaningful relationship between two people. Genuine and deep submission comes from trust, respect and deep connection.

Submission is something evoked

When a leader behaves nobly, it enhances and evokes the submission of another. A leader's actions greatly determine their servant's submission.

Submission is humility

A true servant is humble and teachable, accepting that they must take instructions and execute and implement them strictly in accordance with the leader's wishes. True strength lies in submission, in dedicating your life with devotion to something beyond yourself.

Submission is out of love

Submission is a by-product of respect. Loyalty should naturally follow from both. It is an honour to serve those you love and respect. A submitted servant recognizes and acknowledges and respects the authority of their leader and their leader's vision.

Submission should be qualified

However, it is crucial that you discern and recognize when submission to a leader is obsessive, unbalanced, and blind. If you do not do this, your submission will lead you as a servant to accept a path that may lead to destruction.

A Cautious Caveat

Notwithstanding the above, your submission must be voluntary; it must not be elicited by coercion.

"The doctrine of blind obedience and unqualified submission to any human power, whether civil or ecclesiastical, is the doctrine of despotism" **(Angelina Grimke).**

3. SELFLESSNESS

"It's when you're acting selflessly that you are at your bravest" **(Veronica Roth).**

"He must increase, but I must decrease." **(John 3:30)**

Selflessness is others-oriented

A true servant is, by nature, selfless because they will always put their leader's and other peoples' needs before their own. Selflessness means being others-oriented and not self-oriented. It means being focused and concerned more with the needs and welfare of others than your own.

Selflessness removes competition

Selflessness is an essential key to a successful relationship because it removes all forms of negative competition between a servant. A selfless servant will put their leader first.

"The greatest achievement is selflessness, the greatest worth is self-mastery, the greatest quality is seeking to serve others" (**Atisa Dipakara Srijnana**).

Selflessness is devoid of personal agendas

Selflessness is serving without looking for any personal gain or seeking to fulfil any selfish agenda. A servant is not self-absorbed or self-centred; they are devoid of selfish ambitions and selfish interests.

"Selfless giving unto others represents one's true wealth" (**John M. Huntsman**).

Selflessness is a strength

Selflessness is a strength not a weakness, because it requires you to resist the normal tendency to put yourself first. This is contrary to human nature.

Selflessness is maturity

Being selfless is a sign of maturity and a mark of your security in who you are. You can only rise to serve others selflessly, without a fear of feeling devalued, when you are secure.

Selflessness must come with self-care

However, beware of extreme selflessness that is motivated by false humility and from a sense of immaturity and low self-esteem. You must also love yourself and be kind to yourself, practicing self-care when sacrificing your own desires for the betterment of others. Beware of being taken advantage of and becoming a doormat, of becoming a bad steward of resources because of your attempts to appear selfless.

Beware of misplaced selflessness

Remember, even suicide bombers believe they are acting selflessly.

A Cautious Caveat

You must never confuse true selflessness with denying yourself to destruction. Do not give yourself to servanthood at the expense of your health. This is foolishness and does not benefit anyone. Unbalanced selflessness comes from seeking approval and validation from others. This can often lead to burnout and more serious ailments.

4. COMMITMENT

"There are only two options regarding commitments, you are either in or out." **(Pat Riley)**

A deep connection

Commitment arises out of being deeply connected to someone or something. A true servant will possess this trait.

A deep passion

Commitment comes out of a deep passion for your leader's vision. Without this, you will struggle to be committed. Your passion cements your commitment.

Commitment is action

You must have a readiness to execute and implement the tasks you have been given because commitment must be seen not just heard.

"Commitment leads to action. Action brings the dream closer." **(Marica Wieder)**

Commitment is consistent

Commitment also entails being consistent in and out of season, without faltering, being erratic or irregular.

Commitment is embracing

Commitment requires that you embrace the cause. You cannot truly be committed to that which you have not embraced, accepted, and understood.

Commitment is an investment

Commitment is being fully engaged and vested - mind, body, and soul.

"Motivation is what gets you started. Commitment is what keeps you going" **(Jim Rohn).**

Commitment is a sign of self-expression

Your commitment is expressed in your unrelenting pursuit of your goal. It is your commitment to excellence that will enable you to attain the success that you seek.

"Stay committed to your decisions but stay flexible in your approach" **(Tony Robbins).**

A Cautious Caveat

It is worth noting that your commitment in serving the leader must be proportionate to the other responsibilities in your life. Your commitment to one must not become a sorrow to others, such as your family.

5. OBEDIENCE

"Obedience to lawful authority is the foundation of manly character."
(**Robert E. Lee**)

Defining obedience

Obedience means being subservient and submissive to another's authority, being dutiful, biddable, deferential, and respectful to another's instructions. Obedience derives from a Latin word meaning leaning towards someone in order to listen to them. You cannot truly obey without listening to and understanding your instructions.

Obedience is a choice

Real obedience is voluntary. It is a conscious choice motivated by factors such as love, respect, honour, and trust.

"True obedience is true freedom" (**Henry Ward Beecher**).

Obedience requires competence

Obedience requires the performance, execution, discharging and fulfilment of instructions efficiently and competently, using the required skills. This will entail a sacrifice.

"Obedience brings success; exact obedience brings miracles" (**Russell M. Nelson**).

True obedience is prompt

Delayed obedience amounts to disobedience. An obedient servant will not procrastinate or delay in the execution of instructions from their leader.

Obedience is full compliance

Obedience means complying with an instruction, order or request from another person - not just complying but complying fully and comprehensively to all the instructions given, not just a portion of them.

Obedience is yielding

An obedient servant is yielded, pliable, amenable, malleable and docile to the instructions and directions from another. They do not harbour or exhibit resistance or stubbornness. This requires humility and sincerity.

Obedience is not totally blind

However, beware of the doctrine of blind and unqualified obedience to a leader who has lost their legitimacy and authenticity and who has become a tyrant or a dictator. Their actions may lead to serious destruction.

A Cautious Caveat

While the above remains true, your obedience to a leader must never override your obedience to God and the law of the land. A case in point is where a lawyer instructs his clerk not to pay taxes. This is common in those workplaces where unscrupulous employers instruct their employees to evade taxes, forge documents, defraud clients, or cook the books. If the employee refuses, they are considered disobedient. In such cases, you must stand up for what is right, follow your conscience and, where necessary, choose to walk away. Joseph's refusal to obey Mrs Potiphar's immoral wishes - his decision to run away - is an example of doing the right thing (Genesis 39).

6. TRUSTWORTHINESS

"Trust is always earned, not given." **(R. Williams)**

Trust is authentic

Trust means being upright, principled, ethical, and incorruptible, no matter what the temptation. A trustworthy servant is without deception or guile.

Trustworthiness requires courage

By this, we mean the courage to do the right thing on all occasions, irrespective of any opposition or persecution, or the consequences.

Trustworthiness is unequivocal

Let your 'yes' be 'yes' and your 'no' be 'no.' You should not be unstable or indecisive but clear and unequivocal in your actions and deliberations.

Trustworthiness is making your word your bond

Being trustworthy means that you keep your word and promises, irrespective of the cost.

Trustworthiness is complete truth

It means telling the whole truth, not being economical with the truth.

"Trustful people are the pure at heart, as they are moved by the zeal of their own trustworthiness" **(Criss Jami)**

Trustworthiness is confidentiality

It is the ability not to disclose matters entrusted to you but to keep private what is private.

Trustworthiness is being reliable

It means you can be counted upon to get the job done competently and on time. A true servant is dependable, accountable, and ready to be answerable without blame-shifting or giving excuses.

7. CONSISTENCY

"Consistency is the foundation of virtue." **(Francis Bacon).**

Consistency harmonizes

A good servant must not be unstable, erratic, or conflicted, but must sing with a consistent and harmonious voice, not producing a cacophony of contradictions.

Consistency is a standard

It means maintaining a standard and a quality in what you do and how you do it, in and out of season, so that your leader and their vision maintain high levels of credibility.

Consistency builds trust

Being consistent will enable you to build trust among those who are following your leader and their vision, thereby preserving the integrity of both.

Consistency births excellence

Excellence is born out of consistent, positive habits and actions because whatever you do repeatedly well will only increase in its excellence.

Consistency shapes destinies

It is not what you do once-in-a-while that shapes your life but what you do consistently.

The secret to your future is hidden in your daily routine.

Consistency is focused multitasking

A true servant is focused and stable even when presented with many tasks.

Consistency is moral strength.

A servant who is consistent is a strong servant because they have mastered the art of self-discipline. They have learned to exhibit tenacity by maintaining their consistency.

Cautious Caveat

While the pros of being consistent are obvious, there are also cons, as when you become too rigid in your ways and completely unable to be flexible when the need arises. In such a case, consistency can hold you back because it can amount to pride ("we've always done it this way before!") and this produces negative consequences. If, for instance, you become consistent in focusing on the wrong thing, or going in the wrong direction, then that consistency can become a negative instead of a positive. Consistency therefore must be a focus on the right things, the right way and the right time, and it must be a focus on the majors and not on the minors.

Thought-Provoking Questions For Discussion

1. What challenges have you had, if any, in remaining loyal in your servanthood?

2. What challenges, if any, have you encountered in submitting to authority while you are serving?

3. Were you always selfless in your servanthood or have you had to work on it? If so, how?

4. Do you consider yourself a committed person once you embark on a cause or do you struggle with commitment?

5. On a scale of 1-10, how would you rate your obedience to authority during servanthood (10 being the most positive)?

6. On a scale of 1-10, where would you rate your trustworthiness in your servanthood?

7. Are you a consistent person and, if not, what challenges do you have with being consistent?

THE 7 HEARTS OF A TRUE SERVANT

The heart is the core of who you are as a person. The heart is the seat of your emotions. It is synonymous with affection. The heart is the locus of your physical and spiritual being. It represents the "central wisdom of feeling as opposed to the head-wisdom of reason." It is made up of compassion and understanding, and it is both life-giving and complex. The heart is a symbol for love. It is central to what it means to be human. That being the case, you may sometimes find, due to circumstances, stress or pressure, that you are not always operating with a pure, jovial, warm, brave and undivided heart, especially when you are called to embrace the hardships of servanthood. A case in point is that of Jacob and Laban. No matter how right Jacob's heart was, Laban consistently went out of his way to frustrate him and render his servanthood a sorrow instead of a blessing.

The Sevens

1. AN OPEN-RECEPTIVE HEART

"Being receptive, being able to listen openly and well, is a crucial skill for creative problem-solving." **(Paul A. Kaufman)**

Open to teaching

A true servant must have a heart that is open and receptive to teaching and direction. This is essential because servanthood requires you to be led.

Open to rebuke

Your heart must be open to correction. You must be able to handle rebukes with the right attitude, even to the point of welcoming it as a benefit to your personal growth and development.

"As you get older and you realize you really don't know as much as you think you know, you listen more. Because then you think, now I need to be more receptive to the things I don't know. That's how you learn" **(Phil Keoghan).**

Rebuke is not rejection

A true servant does not mistake a rebuke for rejection because they are fully assured of their leader's good faith and intentions.

A closed heart has no understanding

The opposite of an open heart is a closed heart that is slow to understand and that disregards instructions. God gives up on dull hearts that refuse to understand (Isaiah 6:10).

An open-heart bears fruit

An open heart is one that readily receives and retains instructions. It consequently bears fruit, displaying true productivity.

An open heart is innovative

A servant with an open and receptive heart is not closed to new ways of doing things. People with open hearts are often innovative and progressive

An open heart is an honest heart

When your heart is open it means that there is accountability and transparency.

2. A PURE HEART

"Speaking the truth is the main attribute of a pure hearted person." *(Eraldo Banovac)*

A pure heart has no hidden agenda

A good servant will be pure and clean, without hidden agenda, undefiled by hidden motives. They will possess a truthful, genuine, sincere, and childlike innocence.

A pure heart is a healed heart

A pure heart is one healed of hurts from the past that so often hinder our ability to be secure in who we are and trustworthy in what we do.

A pure heart has no toxins

A pure heart has no grudges or ill will, no anger, bitterness, resentment, jealousy, envy. A pure heart is a forgiving heart. The servant's heart should not be burdened by toxic emotions such as unforgiveness.

"A pure heart does not demean the spirit of an individual. Instead, it compels the individual to examine his spirit" **(Criss Jami).**

A pure heart is a purged heart

A pure heart has been purged and purified of all evil and carnality.

"A pure heart begets pure thoughts" **(Lailah Gifty Akita).**

A pure heart is a light heart

The servant's heart must be light, unencumbered by unnecessary or strange burdens, weights, griefs, sorrows etc.

A pure heart is a prayerful heart

With a pure hearted servant, what you see is what you get. Your life of prayer cleanses you from insincerity and creates a lightness in your entire being.

"Prayer keeps the heart pure" (**Lailah Gifty Akita**).

A pure heart keeps your speech clean

Jesus said, "The mouth will bring forth what is in the heart" (**Matthew 12:34**).

Guard your heart with all due diligence for out of it flows the issues of life. "Out of the abundance of the heart the mouth speaks" (**Proverbs 4:23-27**).

3. A BRAVE HEART

A brave heart endures anything threatening and is fearless in the presence of danger.

"I want a courageous heart. A heart that does the right thing even when it's afraid" (**Lauren Gaskill**).

A brave heart is heroic

It is audacious, gallant, gutsy and adventurous. It is courageous and bold, tenacious and resolute. It engages in exploits without fear of failure.

A brave heart is not faint

A true servant's heart is emotionally strong, able to withstand the harshest of challenges.

"The only thing greater than power of the mind is the courage of the heart" (**John Nash**).

A brave heart is well shielded

A servant's heart must not be easily offended or wounded; it must be well guarded.

A brave heart is a warrior's heart

A true servant is a courageous warrior and a fighter, a defender and protector of their leader and their leader's vision.

A brave heart is a giant slayer

The true servant has a heart that goes on the offensive and not the defensive. They have the heart of a giant-slayer, believing they can overcome any obstacle.

A brave heart protects

A servant with a timid or cowardly heart will be a serious hazard to their leader's life and vision. Brave hearts are protective hearts.

4. A BIG HEART

"Wherever you go, go with all your heart." **(Confucius)**

A big heart is without selfish agenda

The big heart is charitable and generous; it loves to give in full measures, without expecting anything in return.

A big heart is an accommodating heart

Such a heart is forbearing, forgiving, always ready to give people the benefit of doubt.

A big heart is noble

A big heart is gracious, noble, and very considerate.

A big heart gives big

A big heart delights in giving sacrificially and generously, not only in terms of resources, but also in time and energy.

A big heart is others-oriented

A big heart is a heart that is selfless, thinking of the needs and welfare of others before their own needs.

A big heart is devoid of self

A big heart is devoid of greed and purged of the desire for excesses or selfish indulgences. It is a heart devoid of and freed from carnal and selfish desires, selfish ambitions, self-absorption, or self-centeredness

A big heart is a people's heart

A big heart will have a great capacity for embracing many people.

5. A WARM HEART

"To keep a warm heart in a cold world is the real victory." **(Marty Rubin)**

A warm heart is compassionate

A loving, kind, sensitive servant, full of compassion, is a true comfort to many because the vision is about people

A warm heart draws people in

It is not hard, stony, and cold. It is not mean, hostile, or cruel. It does not push people away, nor does it hurt them. It does not undermine the leader's vision.

A warm heart feels for people

A warm heart easily perceives the needs and pain of others and responds sensitively.

"A smile's warmth comes from the fire within the heart" **(Anthony T. Hincks).**

A warm heart is a deep well to draw from

A warm heart is not shallow. It is deep well from which others can draw great strength.

A warm heart trusts

A warm heart is friendly and caring towards people, extending trust and opportunities for bonding.

"True compassion means not only feeling another's pain but also being moved to help relieve it" (**Daniel Goleman**).

A warm heart loves

A true servant serves because they love the person they are serving. They love the vision they are serving. They love those who benefit from the vision and above all they love God.

A warm heart reaches diverse people

A warm heart has the capacity to impact and transform lives because it can accommodate the diversity in people and love even the unlovable.

6. AN UNDIVIDED HEART

An undivided heart is not conflicted

An undivided heart is one which is committed, wholeheartedly not half-heartedly.

An undivided heart is stable

A divided heart is unstable, indecisive, easily distracted and swayed and manipulated by wrong desires and forces. It is rebellious and unable to contain instructions.

An undivided heart is focused

A true servant's heart is a heart that is single, not double-minded.

An undivided heart remains on course

A servant's heart does not dilute its energy by looking at many things but keeps focused on the main thing.

An undivided heart will not betray

The divided heart will execute their duties negligently rather than diligently.

An undivided heart is a healed heart

An undivided heart is whole, not scarred and marred by unfaced pain and wounds.

An undivided heart is strong

A servant whose heart is undivided will be strong in their convictions.

7. A JOVIAL HEART

"To serve is beautiful, but only if it is done with joy and a whole heart and a free mind." **(Pearl S. Buck)**

A jovial heart cheers

A servant with a jovial heart is joyful, positive, optimistic, of good cheer because they enjoy serving willingly. Such people are jubilant. They choose to be joyful every day.

A jovial heart is sunshine

Such a servant sees the bright side of things, no matter how daunting the circumstances. A joyful heart is like the sunshine of God's love, the hope of eternal happiness.

A jovial heart is strength

A servant with a jovial heart is strengthened by the joy in their heart and remains energetic throughout their servanthood.

A jovial heart is contagious

A servant who has a jovial heart has contagious joy. This servant ministers to their fellow workers and to others who are downcast. A depressed, despondent servant will have a negative influence and will discourage rather than encourage their leader.

A jovial heart is passionate

A servant serving without a joyful heart shows they have no passion for their work so the level of their performance will be compromised.

A jovial heart is not oppressed

Lack of a joyful heart shows that the servant is serving unwillingly, like a slave. "The miracle is not that we do this work, but that we are happy to do it" (Mother Teresa).

A jovial heart is full of love

A joyful heart is the normal result of a heart burning with love.

"Joy is the net of love by which you can catch souls. She gives most who gives joy" **(Mother Teresa).**

Thought Provoking Questions For Discussion

1. Do you feel that your heart is open and receptive? If not, what hinders you from opening your heart?

2. Would you consider yourself a pure-hearted person? Are there times you have not felt pure-hearted? If so, what were the reasons?

3. Do you consider that you have a big heart? If so, how has it enhanced your servanthood?

4. Do you believe you serve with a jovial heart? Has it made a difference in enhancing your servanthood?

5. Are you a warm-hearted person? If so, how has this enriched your servanthood?

6. What factors, if any, have caused you at times to serve with a divided heart?

7. Do you feel you serve courageously and bravely? If not, what holds you back?

THE 7 COMPETENCIES OF A TRUE SERVANT

"If you think you can do it, that's confidence. If you can do it, that is competence" (**Morris Code**).

Competence forms one out of the two key pillars of servanthood, the other being character. Competence comprises capability, proficiency, adaptability, dexterity, expertise, aptitude, the possession of required skills, knowledge, qualification, intellectual ability, and so on. Often these are not visible until a task is completed.

"The test of true competence is the end result" (L. Ron Hubbard).

Competence is the ability to do something skillfully, efficiently, and successfully. A true servant must be competent to undertake the tasks and duties required. They will possess the relevant knowledge and skills, seeking to improve continuously. Such a person is diligent, resourceful, and hardworking. *"Diligence leads to competence"* (Jeffrey Benjamin).

However, you will not have all the competencies in place when you start your servanthood; they will develop over time. Your task is to work on your own growth and development. When Solomon was building the temple, he looked for the most skilled workers and craftsmen (2 Chronicles 2:5-7).

In what areas does the servant need to be competent?

The following seven capabilities are essential for anyone who wants to excel in effective and successful servanthood:

1. SKILLED

"Skill and confidence are an unconquered army." (George Herbert).

"Practice gives you skills. Skills give you competence. Competence gives you confidence" (Woody Miller).

Mastery in his skill

A servant must have the relevant skill sets so that there is no doubt that they have the necessary qualifications to perform the task at hand.

Skills of high quality

A skill is the ability to do something well and with expertise, and to maintain a high quality and high standards.

Lack of skills is a liability

A servant without the necessary skills will be a liability to their leader because they will exhibit weak performance. This will lead to loss and prejudice the vision.

Must invest in skills

A good leader will invest in training a willing servant to acquire the required skills. Provided the servant has a good character, they can be trained because they will be receptive and teachable. Stephen Covey, in his famous book *The 7 Habits of Highly Effective People*, extols the virtue of sharpening your saw through constant training.

The skill of decision making

Making good and right decisions is a skill, and a skill in turn is the combination of what you know from experience and what you have learned in theory.

"Skill is the unified force of experience, intellect and passion in their operation" (John Ruskin).

Everyone has a special skill

Each person needs to identify that special aptitude which will enable them to attain a higher life within their daily existence. There can be no nobler aim.

"Only a man who is exceptionally skilful can stand before kings" (Sunday Adelaja).

You are skilled for your call

Your calling is your unique area of expertise. Your skills point to your true calling.

2. EFFECTIVENESS

Effectiveness is the ability to carry out your work with such a level of quality that you bear fruit in excellent overall performance. It also means being responsive to the needs of your teammates and the issues they value most.

Effectiveness includes the proper use of your resources and the use of other tools available to you such as technology, human resources, knowledge and so on. Effectiveness does not come by default, but it comes by an intentional dedication to being effective. In this, you will require regular self-assessment to take stock of your strengths and weaknesses. Knowing where you fall short does not make you weak; it allows you to collaborate with your co-servants who have the abilities that you do not in order to achieve the common goal. It means knowing how people really perceive you and having honest communication so you can improve.

Effectiveness will require you to be passionate and focused in your tasks and assignments. It will also require you to know the leader you are serving, their vision, the organization, the overall purposes and goals, and the agreed strategies to achieve those goals.

You must also know your team members and how they fit into the big picture and the part each plays in advancing the vision, so that the leader and the organization grows and thrives. In other words, full knowledge of everything pertaining to your servanthood, both internally and externally, is crucial to your effectiveness.

Normal effectiveness, of course, comes as a result of you being skilled and competent in what you are undertaking. *Maximum* effectiveness, however, will arise from you operating in your area of greatest strength.

Being effective differs from being efficient in that being effective is doing the right thing whereas being efficient is doing the thing right, whether those things are the right things to do or not. Think of effectiveness when dealing with people and efficiency when dealing with things. Effectiveness is better measured by results over time.

Effectiveness has been best summarized by Stephen Covey in *The 7 Habits of Highly Effective People*. He says that the following seven "habits" mark out those who are highly effective in their lives and work:

a) Being proactive (thinking through your response in every situation)
b) Beginning with the end in mind (seeing the whole picture)
c) Putting first things first (prioritizing)
d) Thinking win-win (being ready to be flexible and compromise)
e) Seeking first to understand then being understood (empathetic listening),
f) Synergy (the power of collaboration)
g) Sharpening the saw (constant self-growth and improvement).

3. RESOURCEFUL

"A resourceful person can see opportunity when others only see obstacles." (Garrett Gunderson)

Open-minded

This means the ability to find quick and clever ways to overcome difficulties, exercising initiative, having the tools to come up with ingenious solutions, and the ability to think creatively and outside the box.

Persistent

This means the ability to continually apply your problem-solving abilities, adapting to new and adverse circumstances with high levels of commitment over the long haul.

Proactive

Great decision-making skills are manifested in the ability to anticipate outcomes ahead of time, and then use your resources wisely in meeting the challenges ahead.

Self-assured

The true servant can make decisions promptly and wisely, even under stress because they are self-assured and have high levels of what is known as stress tolerance.

Imaginative and creative

The resourceful servant possesses the ability to process information, to learn quickly, to think outside the box, and respond in quick-witted, innovative ways to every new problem that their leader and their organization faces.

Self-motivated

A true servant must be highly self-motivated. They do not need to be pushed to perform and can be relied upon to work well without supervision, monitoring or micromanaging. The truly resourceful servant is a self-starter. They do not need to be kick started into life and action by their manager's jump-leads.

Hopeful

Such a servant is optimistic and always sees the positive view of situations. "Tap into resourcefulness; unleash creativity; progress will follow" (Anonymous).

4. VALUABLE

"Try not to become a man of success, but rather try to become a man of value." (Albert Einstein).

Value is beneficial

You must add value by being of great use. You do this by offering good advice and being beneficial to the leader's vision.

Value is relevant

You must be a relevant component in the scheme of things. Being valuable as a servant means being relevant to the leader and the leader's vision almost to a point of being indispensable, without that being something you use against your leader.

Value is harnessed skills

A wise servant will seek to become more and more valuable in their servanthood by constantly sharpening their skills through self-growth and development.

Value is preserved treasure

A servant's ability to multi-task wisely and diversely becomes precious treasure. Of such a person, the leader will often say that they are "priceless".

Value earns more

Becoming more and more valuable is the key to promotion. A wise servant will therefore not seek to earn more but to become more valuable.

"Always do more than what you get paid for. It makes you a valuable person" (Jim Rohn).

Value is in Self

Learn to work harder on yourself than anywhere else because it is by being valuable and more empowered that you will make the difference.

Value is focus

Being valuable requires being focused and deliberate because you can only become valuable by design and not by default.

"The most valuable person is the one who cherishes the value in others" (Ron Kaufman).

5. EFFECTIVE COMMUNICATION

Effective communication is about hearing what the other person is saying.

"To effectively communicate, we must realize that we are all different in the way we perceive the world and use this understanding as a guide to our communication with others" (Tony Robbins)

A servant's ability to communicate effectively is key to their ability to serve their leader.

Whether their communication is verbal, non-verbal, visual, or written, a servant must do so with coherence, emotional intelligence, clarity, friendliness, empathy, and respect. Knowing the *what*, the *why*, the *where*, the *who*, the *how* of communication is crucial. A servant who communicates effectively will preserve and safeguard the leader from unnecessary and damaging misunderstanding.

What you are communicating is crucial because the ability to package and sieve the content of your communication will impact your ability to communicate effectively.

Why you are communicating is important because these reasons will help you distinguish what is important from what is merely informative or useful.

Where you are communicating – your environment and atmosphere, private or public - will greatly affect how your audience receives what you are saying.

How you communicate is about your tone, emotion, and body posture.

The *Who* you are communicating with means assessing the recipient of your message - their age, gender, and temperament, and so on. The mode you choose will be determined by the person with whom you are communicating.

6. ART OF SELF-DISCIPLINE

"Discipline is the bridge between goals and accomplishment." (Jim Rohn)

I discipline my body and bring it into subjection, lest, when I have preached to others, I myself should become disqualified. **(1 Corinthians 9: 27)**

Self-discipline has willpower

Self-discipline is the ability to make yourself do what you should whether you feel like it or not. It is a test of character and willpower.

Self-discipline conquers

You can never conquer a mountain until you have first conquered yourself.

Self-discipline is hard work

Self-discipline overcomes lethargy, laziness, procrastination, fear, and self-doubt. It requires you to become the master and not the slave of your thoughts and emotions.

Self-discipline has a reward

Self-discipline is key to delivering desired results. It is connecting today's actions to tomorrow's rewards.

"For every disciplined effort there is a multiple reward" (Jim Rohn).

Self-discipline has a process

Self-discipline is developed over time. It is a process. Whenever you fail, you should avoid self-condemnation and instead get up and keep trying.

Self-discipline is the result of your free choice

The word "self" in self-discipline highlights the fact that the discipline you develop happens as a result of your choice, not another person's coercion. It is developed by design, not by default.

"If you will discipline yourself to make your mind self-sufficient, you will thereby be least vulnerable to injury from the outside" *(Critias of Athens).*

7. NOTABLE

Notable is tested

A notable servant's capabilities will continue to be harnessed and improved. They will always have their skills tested and proven.

Notable is authentic

When notable servants are tested and come out the other side with a glowing report, their servanthood is rightly deemed to be the real deal.

Notable is knowledgeable

Notable servants are prized for the knowledge they have acquired through experience not just through education, through testing not just through theory.

Notable is remarkable

Notable servanthood is something unusual, precious, outstanding, striking, impressive, exceptional, noteworthy.

Notable entails multitasking

A notable servant can carry out multiple instructions without getting confused or distracted.

Notable entails going ahead of the pack

A notable servant is way ahead of others in both character and competence. They stand out as exemplary and above average.

Notable has a niche

Notable also means that a servant has marked out a niche for themselves. They become renowned for their competence and character in this specific area and their servanthood becomes an example for many to emulate and a lesson from which many can learn.

Thought Provoking Questions for Discussion

1. Did you consider your skill sets when discovering your call and your sphere of servanthood?

2. What do you consider more important, being efficient or being effective?

3. Have you always been resourceful in your servanthood or did you have to work on it and, if so, how?

4. Have you always been valuable, or did you have to work on it and, if so, how?

5. Do you consider yourself an effective communicator? If not, how has this affected your servanthood? How can you improve it?

6. On a scale of 1-10 (10 being the best, the highest), how would you rate your self-discipline? Which areas are most challenging for you?

7. Do you believe that your servanthood so far has been notable? If not, which ways do you think can make it notable?

Chapter 3

THE PURPOSE OF A SERVANT

Discovering Your Call to Serve and the Functions It Entails

"You were put on this earth to achieve your greatest self, to live out your purpose and do it courageously"
(Steve Maraboli)

Chapter Outline

The 7 Functions of Servanthood

1. To Promote & To Support
2. To Interpret & Articulate the Vision
3. To Be Available & Accessible
4. To Protect & Guard
5. To Encourage and Strengthen
6. To Represent
7. To Execute & Implement the Vision

The 7 Right Attitudes of a Servant

1. A Long-Suffering Attitude
2. An Excellence Attitude
3. A Diplomatic Attitude
4. A Team Player Attitude
5. An Others-Oriented Attitude
6. A Positive Attitude
7. A Self-Confident Attitude

The 7 Endowments of a Servant

1. Endowed with Wisdom
2. Endowed with Discernment
3. Endowed with Intervention, Interception & Intercession
4. Endowed with A Radical Faith
5. Endowed with A Proactive Attitude
6. Endowed with Creativity
7. Endowed for Followership

INTRODUCTION

Discovering that you have a call to serve is not enough on its own; you must first consider the functions and obligations of that call, namely your roles, responsibilities, duties, assignments, and tasks. These relate to performance and to the delivery of results, which means that you must exhibit and continually harness your competence. Furthermore, you must understand the limits of your mandate in the performance of your functions and obligations. Your empowerment to serve comes with set boundaries and parameters; this is to ensure that you do not exceed your use of power or authority.

In your role as a servant, you must acknowledge your liability, the extent to which you will be held accountable for loss and damage in the performance of your obligations and in the exercise of your mandate, your power and your authority.

A servant's obligations, mandates and liabilities will develop and be subject to periodic review as the vision of your leader evolves and progresses.

Discerning and understanding the different dispositions of your leader and knowing how to respond and relate to your leader will be critical factors in your ability to carry out your functions.

As a modern-day servant, your functions are comparable to those of the Old Testament armour-bearer. The armour-bearer was a servant under the authority of a leader or a master. In today's terms, the word "master" refers to managers, employers, CEOs, ministers in a cabinet, bishops, pastors, associate pastors and so forth.

The armour-bearer and their master flowed in the same anointing. Both fought and wrestled with the same enemies. Armour-bearers did not just hold shields; they were as skilled as their master in the heat of battle. Jonathan's armour-bearer was called to help shoulder his master's load, to bear up and carry the burden with him.

A seasoned armour-bearer or servant is therefore not a helpless helper but an effective and highly valued assistant.

An armour-bearer was originally chosen to be a military aide to a king. They were chosen for their abilities and skills. As they worked for their masters, these competencies were sharpened.

The title "armour-bearer" is therefore synonymous with personal assistant. It refers to someone who is more than a menial slave. Armour-bearers normally move on to the calling God has for them, as David did. He became Saul's armour-bearer (1 Samuel 16). He stood with his king – an important and valuable position. This gave David the opportunity to learn how kings conduct themselves as he grew into his own royal destiny.

Although an armour-bearer was lower in honour than a leader, they always went ahead and in front of a leader and stood between the leader and the Goliaths they were called to confront (1 Samuel 17). Armour-bearers are therefore like presidential bodyguards, tasked to give their lives for their leader if the situation dictates. Armour-bearers, both then and now, are mandated to defend their masters or leaders.

Armour-bearers were also expected to execute their leader's orders in full, no matter how extreme. For example, in 1 Samuel 31:4, King Saul ordered his armour-bearer to kill him. King Abimelech did the same. Note that King Saul's armour-bearer refused; he killed himself when King Saul died because he regarded it as a dishonour to survive when the person he had been defending had died. Armour-bearers had to be willing and ready to die with their master. In our day, this means being prepared to endure hardships. Servants must be willing to defend their leader and the vision, protecting their leader's reputation and integrity by dealing with rumours or lies.

In Old Testament times, the master also entrusted his life to the armour-bearer. Jonathan consulted his armour-bearer because he valued his opinion. Armour-bearing is accordingly deeper than servitude. Two are better than one. An armour-bearer fighting alongside their master is a formidable force, an example of spiritual synergy. The armour-bearer had their master's back, something that required deep loyalty.

Armour-bearers also had to be able to dot the 'i's and cross the 't's; in other words, to ensure that all was well, that no stone had been left unturned, so that the leader was not caught unprepared and thereby shamed.

Armour-bearers had to place their own desires and goals beneath those of the master they were serving and submit to the master's vision. They had to suspend their own agendas and focus on their master's agenda.

Armour-bearers had to protect their masters by anticipating and spotting the snares and traps of the enemy. Then they would warn and shield their master against disaster by anticipating attacks designed to discredit the master.

Understanding the purpose of your servanthood will entail you receiving a brief or job description that outlines exactly what is expected of you.

When we serve with excellence, we bring honour to our authorities. The leader can only look good and make strides forward if their servants serve well, are focused, and avoid infighting. A servant's success or failure reflects on the leader. CEOs are answerable to boards; they serve a bigger vision designed for the improvement of a nation or society. A leader's furtherment is tied to their servants.

A servant's role is to make their leader look good. A servant must own the agenda/vision of the other and advance it while watching their leader's back. This is important in the marketplace because the corporate world often propagates self-interest and tends to be self-oriented. Climbing the corporate ladder means stepping on others to get to the top while watching your own back. True servanthood is reflected in 1 Samuel 14:1-14, the relationship between Jonathan and his armour-bearer. "I am with you heart and soul," the armour-bearer says.

THE 7 FUNCTIONS OF SERVANTHOOD

The following are the seven functions of a true servant: (1) to promote and support, (2) to interpret and articulate the vision, (3) to execute and implement the vision, (4) to be available, (5) to protect, (6) to strengthen and encourage (7) and to represent.

The 7 Sevens

1. TO PROMOTE AND TO SUPPORT YOUR LEADER

This is the anointing possessed by Aaron and Hur in Exodus 17:12. They were both Moses's servants. They lifted Moses' arms during a time of battle. While Moses's arms remained up, Joshua had the upper hand.

Being in agreement

"When we promote the well-being of others God has placed in our lives, our servanthood glorifies God" (Elizabeth George).

Being in agreement means believing in your leader and owning their vision, agreeing with them and associating yourself with them and their vision. It is impossible with integrity to support or promote a person or a vision that you do not believe in, agree with or associate with. Supporting and promoting your leader requires that you back them up morally, physically, emotionally, and spiritually. It is hard to do this if you do not believe in them or the vision that they are carrying.

A good leader will sometimes consult with you and seek your view and opinion on certain issues. They will go out of their way to show you that they value your input. That said, you must not demand to be consulted or feel entitled to be consulted. When your leader does not consult with you on an issue you should remain submitted and humble. Jonathan consulted his armour-bearer as a sign of how much he valued him and his input.

Being an Advocate

Being an advocate means being a seller and marketer of your leader and their vision. You do this by speaking well and pitching positively, creating awareness, selling, championing, and campaigning for your leader, endorsing and validating their vision. A diligent servant will go out of their way to do these things. They will be consumed by this goal, fulfilling this mandate in and out of season. They will mobilize resources, followers, supporters, and partners for their leader's vision.

Rallying and mobilizing

Servants rally supporters and followers, mobilize donors, sponsors, and resources to feed and nourish the vision.

Bearing burdens

Bearing the burdens of your leader and their vision means standing by them in all seasons. In Exodus 17:12 we read, "When Moses' hands grew tired, they took a stone and put it under him and he sat on it. Aaron and Hur held his hands up, one on one side, one on the other so that his hands remained steady till sunset."

Elevating

Elevating refers to uplifting your leader, adding value to the vision by affirming them and by introducing innovative and progressive concepts. This builds the leader's confidence and advances their calling.

"There is no greater power and support you can give someone than to look them in the eye, and with sincerity/conviction say, 'I believe in you'." (Ken Poirot)

Performing and fulfilling

By performing and fulfilling all your duties promptly, competently, and comprehensively, you advance the leader's cause.

Contributing to success

To support is to aid someone to succeed in their ideas and goals. To promote is to contribute to the progress and growth of a person or a cause. A servant is called to do both.

A Cautious Caveat

It is worth mentioning that your promoting and supporting must be for a person or cause that does not contradict the Word of God, the law of the land or your core values. To promote and support that which is ungodly, illegal, or immoral leads to wrongdoing for which you will find yourself liable.

2. TO INTERPRET AND ARTICULATE YOUR LEADER'S VISION

This is the Joseph anointing. Joseph, as a servant to the Pharaoh, was able to interpret and articulate Pharaoh's dream (Genesis 41).

Unveiling the vision

The vision given by God to a leader will naturally require careful interpretation for accurate execution and implementation. This means that God will endow a true servant with the gift to interpret that vision for their leader.

Keep interpreting as the vision evolves

A visionary leader will continue to receive downloads from the throne room of heaven. These come in the form of night visions and dreams which they will share with their trusted servant. That servant must have the ability to interpret the details and fill in the gaps.

Interpret resources required

While interpreting the vision, a servant will also have to understand the required human and material resources for the vision to be activated and fulfilled. They will need to anticipate what consultancy fees, workers' salaries, and other capital outlays are needed.

Interpreting time lines and pace

They will also need to interpret and come up with a schedule for implementing the vision as well as a time line, sequencing everything that needs to happen, and the pace of progress.

Interpreting the needs of the beneficiaries

They will need to interpret who the beneficiaries of the vision are and to assess their receptivity to the changes required of them.

Interpreting the jurisdiction

They will need to interpret the jurisdiction of the vision. In other words, what regions and spheres the vision seeks to reach and impact. That way they can keep the vision within its scope and mandate.

3. TO BE AVAILABLE AND ACCESSIBLE FOR YOUR LEADER

This is the Elisha anointing we find in 2 Kings chapter2. As a servant of Elijah, Elisha remained present and available to Elijah right up to the end of his master's life. This shows that availability is as important as ability.

Being present

Being available means being permanently present - present physically, emotionally, and mentally. As someone once said: "Don't just be able; make sure you are available. Be present to make a change."

Being ready

Being available means that you are not only present but that you are also ready to serve. You will be ready and equipped with whatever tools you need.

"Your ability will not help you if you do not give your availability" ***(Saji Ijiyemi).***

Giving priority

Being available means that you respect and value your servanthood and you regard this as a priority item on your agenda. As someone has warned, "If you are capable but not available, nature will raise a person with lesser ability to quickly replace you."

Having the right attitude

Being available does not only mean being present and ready; it also demands that you have the right attitude for servanthood, which means not murmuring or complaining. "God does not ask for your ability or inability. He asks only for your availability" (Mary Kay Ash).

Managing other priorities

Being available means managing other priorities in your life (e.g., family), since servanthood may involve long hours and travelling.

Being easily accessible

Being available means being readily accessible, reachable, at your leader's beck and call, easily reachable on the phone. Keeping open lines of communication is crucial.

Being preferable because of availability

When the best option isn't available, leaders opt for anybody who is present. "To a hungry person, every bitter food is sweet; when the preferable is not available, the available becomes preferable" (Israel More).

A Cautious Caveat

Your ability to be available and accessible to the person you are serving must be qualified by and proportionate to your other responsibilities and must be within appropriate boundaries so that you retain your personal privacy. It is unfortunate that sometimes a leader makes the mistake of taking a servant for granted when that servant is always available. At other times, they may even abuse or misuse that availability. The world says, "never be too available for someone otherwise you will lose your importance." The Word of

God says that a servant's availability is firstly unto God. Therefore, keep things in their divine order.

4. TO PROTECT AND GUARD YOUR LEADER

This is the anointing that was upon David's mighty men in 2 Samuel 23:8–38. They made it their call and duty to ensure that David, the light of Israel, was never harmed by their enemies.

Guarding and defending

A leader will be faced with many attacks and battles - physical, verbal, even libellous. These will be directed against their vision and resources, their family and reputation. It is the duty of a brave servant to protect their leader. A brave servant is a giant slayer and one of their main roles is to guard and defend their leader from all manner of attacks and threats, whether internal or external to the organization.

To die protecting

A brave servant should be willing to die defending and protecting their leader and their leader's welfare.

Protecting by shielding

A brave servant should protect their leader by standing in the gap in intercession on behalf of their leader, thereby raising the shield of faith against the enemy.

Protecting with the sword and the Word

In olden days, a brave servant was skilled in the use of the sword for neutralizing their master's enemies. A modern-day servant must be skilled in the use of the Word. A brave servant should be prepared to fight hard and long in protecting their leader.

Protecting with right and left hand

A brave servant must be able to use both their hands in protecting their leader. The right hand symbolizes their physical strength and power, the left their spiritual authority. This means that a servant must have the ability to combine both action and prayer.

Protecting reputation and honour

A brave servant will defend and protect the reputation and honour of their leader and repel every false accusation, slander, libel, and defamation, thereby covering the shame and nakedness of their leader. They must also be able to defend the leader's vision and the resources of that vision.

Protecting by sieving anything negative and harmful

This is the Nehemiah anointing we find in Nehemiah Chapter 1. Nehemiah, the king's cupbearer, tasted the king's food and wine before giving it to the king lest it be harmful. A sensitive servant will protect their leader from receiving information and reports that are negative, discouraging and defiling.

A Cautious Caveat

As a servant willing to defend your leader, you must also check to ensure that your leader is willing to be protected and guarded in the manner you have adopted. This will ensure that in your attempts to do the right thing you do not end up suffocating and smothering your leader, or worse still manipulating and controlling them, hindering well-meaning people from accessing them who could be of benefit to them.

5. TO ENCOURAGE AND TO STRENGTHEN YOUR LEADER

This is the Joshua and Caleb anointing that we find in Numbers 13. Joshua and Caleb were Moses's servants. They passionately believed in Moses and diligently obeyed his instructions, bringing great strength and encouragement to their leader.

"Encourage, lift and strengthen one another. For the positive energy spread to one will be felt by us all. For we are connected, one and all" (Deborah Day).

As iron sharpens iron, so one person sharpens another. Proverbs 27:17

Edifying and building up

Every leader undergoes moments and seasons when they become physically and emotionally worn out, so it is the duty of a good servant to strengthen them by recounting to them their past victories to revive their hope and resolve.

Adding

This means adding to, increasing, and expanding the impact of your leader and their vision. It is all too easy to subtract from a leader's vision. Adding to it requires a much higher level of self-sacrifice and grace.

To equip with knowledge

This means equipping your leader by giving them facts and data that enable them to make decisions that are informed and useful. As Hebrews 10:24 says, "Let us consider how we may spur one another on towards love and good deeds."

Rebuilding broken walls

This means closing the gaps that may have opened during attacks and that may threaten and weaken your leader and their vision.

Firming up

This means reinforcing the structures and systems in your leader's vision to strengthen the foundation of the vision, which may have become cracked and worn over time.

Motivating and affirming

This means to inspire and encourage your leader, restoring their confidence and self-esteem by cheering them up, spurring them on, invigorating them to keep going (Hebrews 10:24).

"Encouragement and hope are the two most powerful qualities any person can provide to another" (Zig Ziglar).

Empowering

This means making your leader more effective and more forceful, serving in a way that increases your leader's strength and makes the vision more powerful, appealing, impactful, and beneficial to those it is intended to reach.

"Be an encourager: when you encourage others, you boost their self-esteem, enhance their self-confidence, make them work harder, lift their spirits and make them successful in their endeavours. Encouragement goes straight to the heart and is always available. Be an encourager. Always" (Roy T. Bennett).

6. TO REPRESENT YOUR LEADER

This is the Aaron anointing we find in Exodus 6:28-30. Aaron, a servant of Moses, became his mouthpiece and voice.

Representing accurate action

A good servant will act on behalf of their leader and their leader's vision by executing instructions strictly in accordance and alignment with their leader's wishes, without distorting or diluting them in any way.

Representing the leader's vision not yours

The servant must not seek to project their own ideas onto the vision without the leader's permission, nor should they ever give others the impression that this is their own vision, or worse still, hijack it as their own.

Representing in a good light

This is the Eliezer anointing in Genesis 24. Eliezer, Abraham's servant, represented Abraham well in sourcing a bride for Abraham's son Isaac. As a good servant, you must speak well of your leader, drawing favour towards them, always shedding good light on them.

Representing with accurate words

An obedient servant will communicate the leader's message accurately and effectively, remembering that they are a messenger responsible for the message, while not being responsible for the reactions of the recipients of that message.

Representing the leader's voice

Your role as a servant is to do the will of your leader and to speak only what you are told to speak. You are your leader's spokesperson.

Representing your leader's brand

A good servant will engage in damage control whenever their leader's brand is threatened. They will always promote the brand of their leader in a positive way.

Representing your leader's behaviour

A servant is an accurate reflection and image of their leader's way of behaving. This is unlike Gehazi who misinterpreted his leader and brought shame on him.

"What you show is what you represent" (Sunday Adelaja).

A Cautious Caveat

You can only represent what you fundamentally agree with. Any representation required of you that does not reflect and align with God's Word, the law of the land or your core values will be difficult for you to implement. Your representation must be authentic.

7. TO EXECUTE AND IMPLEMENT THE VISION OF THE LEADER

This is the Joseph anointing found in Genesis 37. Joseph becomes the servant of Pharaoh after accurately interpreting and articulating the Pharaoh's dream and vision. Joseph was then able to execute and implement that vision during seasons of both famine and plenty.

Diligently and faithfully

The leader shares their vision and a faithful servant embarks on fulfilling all the requisite tasks and assignments for the implementation of that vision faithfully and diligently.

Successfully

To execute is to perform the leader's strategy, instructions, directions, and decisions in such a way as to realize the best possible results and outcome. For example, when a leader like Kenya's President Uhuru birthed and shared his vision of the four pillars, he then released it to his cabinet secretaries, his servants, to execute and implement it to its fulfilment.

Excellently

A good servant will demonstrate 'execution excellence' by listening carefully to instructions and embarking on a definitive process of implementing them.

Authentically

A servant must ensure that they keep the original vision blueprint intact when executing it. They must avoid distorting it or taking credit for it.

Strategic planning

Executing and implementing the leader's vision will mean coming up with strategic ideas and plans, selling them to your team members so that you can implement them together and in unity.

"Plan your execution. Execute your plan" (Anonymous).

Comprehensive execution

Effective execution will require the servant to understand, embrace and own the vision in its entirety so that everyone is able to implement it comprehensively.

Competently

Executing and implementing will also require that the servant and the team members possess the necessary competence in terms of skills, capacity, and abilities.

A Cautious Caveat

Your execution and implementation must be of things that align with the Word of God, the law of the land and your core values. The means must justify the ends.

Thought Provoking Questions for Discussion

1. How instrumental do you believe you have been in promoting and supporting the people and visions you have served? Have there been times when you regret not having been more supportive?

2. What challenges have you encountered, if any, in interpreting and articulating visions you have served? Have there been instances when you misinterpreted or mis-articulated a vision? If so, what were the consequences?

3. What things and people in your life have you had to sacrifice in order to be available in your servanthood? Was it worth it?

4. Are there instances when you suffered personal loss or injury while protecting and guarding those you were serving? If so, how did you feel about that?

5. How have you been able to encourage and strengthen those you were serving when you yourself were feeling discouraged and weak? Have you ever felt that you did not represent those you were serving accurately and adequately? What hindered you from doing so and what effect did it have on the welfare of those you were representing?

6. How do you separate your own voice (views and opinions) from the voice (views and opinions) of the leader and the people you are representing?

7. Have there been times when you have felt you did not have the adequate skills and competencies to fully execute and implement the vision you were serving?

THE 7 RIGHT ATTITUDES OF A SERVANT

To enable you to perform your functions as a servant you must adopt seven right attitudes: attitudes of long-suffering, excellence, diplomacy, selflessness, positivity, self-confidence, and the mentality of the team player. These are the seven right attitudes of a true servant. Attitude here refers to the way a servant behaves mentally, emotionally, and physically. Even your stance and demeanour can speak volumes in various situations and circumstances. So, then, here are the seven right attitudes:

The 7 Sevens

1. A LONG-SUFFERING ATTITUDE

This is the Job anointing we find throughout the *Book of Job*. Job endured and persevered and continued to trust in God.

Not only so, but we also glory in our sufferings, because we know that our suffering produces perseverance; perseverance, character and character hope. (Romans 5:3-4)

Keep serving despite hardships

This long-suffering attitude involves enduring, being patient, having the capacity and the ability to show perseverance in the face of troubles, hardships, difficulties, frustrations, and stressful situations. Being long-suffering is a sign of maturity, showing that a person has what it takes to do the job at hand despite the circumstances, that they have learned to rise above and master adversity no matter how extreme. Such a person is not a seasonal servant but one who is in it for the long haul. They will jump at the chance of offering a helping hand or taking on an additional workload because their purpose is to serve others.

No murmuring, no complaining

This is the ability to endure without complaining or murmuring. A true servant must be able to handle uncomfortable situations while maintaining a good attitude.

Suppose one of you had a servant ploughing or looking after the sheep. Would he say to the servant when he comes in from the field, "Come along now and sit down to eat?" Would he not rather say, "Prepare my supper, get yourself ready and wait on me while I eat and drink; after that you may eat and drink." Would he thank the servant because he did what he was told to do? So, you also, when you have done everything, you were told to do, should say, "We are unworthy servants; we have only done our duty." (Luke 17:7-10)

Trust and faith

The long-suffering attitude is a demonstration that you have a trust and faith that things will work out well in the end, as you do what needs to be done.

And we know that in all things God works for the good of those who love him, who have been called according to his purpose. (Romans 8:28)

Eagle Christian

The long-suffering attitude involves being an "eagle Christian"– someone who knows how to behave like the one who waits on the Lord in the *Book of Isaiah*, renewing their strength in waiting. The art of waiting in this Biblical sense is not a passive thing. It is an active pursuit of God's person and purposes.

"With patience and perseverance, the mountain is conquered" (Lailah Gifty Akita).

Remaining whole and grounded

The long-suffering attitude will require you to develop a high level of emotional intelligence (EQ) in self and social awareness. This will enable you to know how to remain whole without falling apart. It will empower you to remain grounded through each season, no matter how weather-beaten you are.

Self-encouragement

The long-suffering attitude will require you to encourage and strengthen yourself in the Lord in various ways, such as through prayer and positive self-declarations, so that you remain a source of strength to your leader and team members.

Positive Energy

The long-suffering attitude will require you to close your ears to all negative talk, negative energy and to ensure you surround yourself with positive people who have positive energy.

"Whoever is present in your Spring would more than likely have respected your Winter" (Johnnie Dent Jr.).

2. AN EXCELLENCE ATTITUDE

"Excellence is never an accident but the result of intention, sincere effort and intelligent execution. It represents the wise choice of many alternatives- it's a choice not chance" (Aristotle).

A Desire to Excel

The attitude of excellence means having a deep desire to ensure that everything you do is in the best way to achieve optimum results. It means being passionate for the task, having your heart totally in the endeavour. This is much easier when your assignment is in alignment with your area of expertise and skill. When that happens, it increases and enhances your ability to be passionate and your desire to excel.

Clarity of intention

The attitude of excellence means not only having a desire to excel but the ability and capacity to ensure that everything you do is done in the best and highest way to achieve optimum results. Excellence requires integrity, doing the right thing and doing it well, even when no one is looking or watching you.

Having an insight

The attitude of excellence means having insight and knowledge about what is excellent and what is not by researching what is deemed to be excellent and then seeking to apply this in your life as a servant. Having this kind of insight gives you a positive attitude and mind-set to exceed expectations and standards.

Excellence is superiority

The attitude of excellence means the ability to convert what is not excellent into what is excellent with expertise and style. It is benchmarking against yourself; instead of looking outward to measure your excellence, you look inward and demand the best of yourself.

Excellence is quality

The attitude of excellence means using quality products and skilled servanthood to ensure an excellent outcome. It is giving the task and assignment your personal attention as opposed to carelessly delegating it.

Creative and innovative

The attitude of excellence means being creative and innovative in ideas and concepts and in the execution of these in serving your leader and their vision. Beware of the fear of others; this may cause you to lower your standards because you will worry that your excellence threatens those who are mediocre.

Excellence is outstanding

The attitude of excellence means doing things above and beyond the expectations of your leader, always going the extra mile. The true goal of excellence is to do the best you can with what you have at every moment.

"Excellence is the result of caring more than others think is wise, risking more than others think is safe, dreaming more than others think is practical and expecting more than others think is possible" **(Ronnie Oldham).**

3. A DIPLOMATIC ATTITUDE

This is the Nehemiah anointing (in *The Book of Nehemiah*) where, despite provocations and aggravations by the likes of Sanballat and Tobias, who were trying to sabotage his anointing, Nehemiah reacted with great skill to outwit and silence their evil schemes, and without having to resort to dramatic confrontational tactics.

The soothing tongue is a tree of life, but a perverse tongue crushes the spirit. (Proverbs 15:4)

In handling situations

A shrewd servant is diplomatic, having the ability to be sensitive in dealing with situations and the wisdom to achieve peaceful resolutions to facilitate discussion, to help resolve issues amicably and without acrimony.

Good people skills

Servanthood will inevitably involve people. A diplomatic servant will therefore possess excellent social skills to safeguard the interests of their leader and the welfare of their people without damaging relationships or alienating others. A diplomatic servant understands that the people who follow a leader – whether this leader operates in the church sphere or in the realm of government and politics - are a great asset and their motto in dealing with them is "Handle with Care."

A gentle answer turns away wrath, but a harsh word stirs up anger. (Proverbs 15:1)

Skilled in dispute resolution

A diplomatic servant will be able to mediate and arbitrate wisely during disputes between people. They will know how to leave both sides satisfied with a solution that is mutually beneficial. They will help people with differences to find common ground.

Skilled in handling the team

A diplomatic servant will handle and manage his co-workers and team members expertly and wisely to guard against dissent and rebellion from within. If a servant does not possess a diplomatic attitude, their leader may suffer irreparable damage.

To answer before listening, that is folly and shame. (Proverbs 18:13)

Skilled at giving feedback

A diplomatic servant will always know how to give feedback to their leader, especially negative feedback, in a way that the leader can receive without being offended.

Uncompromised truth

While maintaining a diplomatic stance, a servant must maintain balance, so that they do not compromise the truth and what is right in seeking peaceful outcomes. Sometimes, falling out may be the only way to maintain the integrity of the leader and their vision.

Handling the leader wisely.

A diplomatic servant will know how to handle their leader's temperament with wisdom, how to manage their leader's expectations, disappointments and frustrations in a way that maintains a healthy relationship between them.

Through patience, a ruler can be persuaded, and a gentle tongue can break a bone. **(Proverbs 25:15)**

4. A TEAM PLAYER ATTITUDE

How good and pleasant it is when God's people live together in unity.
Psalms 133:1

Seeks similar goals

A good servant will possess a team spirit and a feeling of pride and loyalty among his fellow co-workers, seeking similar goals and results.

Team culture

The team-player attitude embraces a shared culture of open, honest communication and interaction. A positive attitude is birthed and maintained through positive self-talk and confessions, listening to positive reports, and rejecting negative ones.

You must be willing to serve everyone

Often, we serve to be seen. We desire the attention and gratitude others bestow upon us when they see our sacrificial service. The more important the person, the greater the feeling of affirmation. Jesus, on the other hand, came to serve everyone, especially the "least."

If anyone gives even a cup of cold water to one of these little ones because he is my disciple, I tell you the truth, he will certainly not lose his reward. (Matthew 10:42)

Common cause

The team-player attitude means showing genuine commitment to the common cause, and this involves demonstrating respect and concern for one another.

"Everyone has a responsibility to not only to tolerate another person's point of view, but also to accept it eagerly as a challenge to your own understanding. And to express those challenges in terms of serving other people" (Arlo Guthrie).

Team unity

A team player does not seek to shine on their own but seeks the unity of the team. Constant team building and bonding sessions will maintain a strong team spirit.

For we are co-workers in God's servanthood; you are God's field, God's building. (1 Corinthians 3:9)

Sharing victories and mistakes alike

A sign of a good servant who is a team player is that they own the mistakes of the team and easily celebrate their own victories as the team's.

5-Star team player

A good team player has five qualities:

- they are always reliable;
- they employ clear and effective communication;
- they go the extra mile;
- they adapt quickly and easily;
- they put the team objectives before their own.

Two are better than one

The success of your leader will be determined largely by a good team, and this means working together in unity, in love and in purpose.

Two are better than one, because they have a good return for their labour. (Ecclesiastes 4:9)

5. AN OTHERS-ORIENTED ATTITUDE

The greatest among you will be your servant. (Matthew 23:11)

Seeking the interest of others

A true servant seeks relational and social influence through affiliation. They always consider the interests of others, and they value working in co-operative and reciprocal ways, putting their leader's interest and the interest of others before their own.

"It is better to serve than be served" (Lailah Gifty Akita).

Do nothing out of selfish ambition or vain conceit but in humility consider others better than yourself. Each of you should look not only to your own interests but also to the interest of others. (Philippians 2:3-4)

Being others-centred is a trait that few people exhibit; often we are mainly concerned with ourselves. Putting others first is the true hallmark of a servant attitude.

Being a good listener

The ability to focus and listen to other peoples' ideas, views, opinions, feelings leads to empathetic listening. When you seek first to understand another before seeking to be understood, you will be a good listener.

Being agreeable

Servants with highly agreeable dispositions are others-oriented while those with low level agreeableness are usually self-oriented.

Demonstrating balance

Being others-oriented does not mean neglecting your own welfare. Maintain the balance between a focus on looking after other's interests and a focus on self-care.

Exhibiting effective servanthood

Serving by its very nature is about people, so an others-oriented servant will prove to be effective in their servanthood.

"The only way you can serve God is by serving other people" (Rick Warren).

God is not unjust; he will not forget your work and the labour you have shown him as you have helped his people and continue to help them. (Hebrews 6:10)

Being naturally authentic

Being others-oriented is not something you can fake because under pressure your real self will emerge. In times of duress, your true nature will surface because the grace was never there to be others-oriented in an authentic way.

Being motivated by love

An others-oriented servant is motivated by a love for people and a sincere desire for their wellbeing and welfare.

6. A POSITIVE ATTITUDE (THE CALEB ANOINTING)

"Optimism is the faith that leads to achievement. Nothing can be done without hope and confidence" (Helen Keller).

A Radical Faith = A Positive Attitude

A progressive servant will possess a positive attitude because a positive attitude will produce positive results. Such people promote faith, ignoring doubts and fear, and are optimistic as opposed to pessimistic. "A pessimist sees the difficulty in every opportunity; an optimist sees the opportunity in every difficulty" (Winston Churchill).

A positive attitude = productivity

A positive attitude promotes confidence and motivation. It boosts self-esteem and hence enhances productivity.

"A positive attitude causes a chain reaction of positive thoughts, events and outcomes. It is a catalyst and it sparks extraordinary results" (Wade Boggs).

A positive attitude = reduced stress

A positive-minded servant will have reduced stress because their positivity eradicates negative energy.

A positive attitude = cheerfulness

A merry heart does good, like medicine, but a broken spirit dries the bones.

"Choosing to be positive and having a grateful attitude is going to determine how you're going to live your life" (Joel Osteen).

A positive attitude is a cheerful spirit working with enthusiasm. (Proverbs 17:22)

A positive attitude never quits

An optimistic servant is not a quitter; they never give up. They see every setback as a setup for learning lessons and moving on undeterred.

Have I not commanded you? Be strong and courageous. Do not be afraid; do not be discouraged, for the Lord your God will be with you wherever you go. (Joshua 1:9)

A positive attitude is contagious

A positive attitude invigorates your leader and team members. A positive attitude keeps a servant healthy physically, emotionally, and mentally.

7. A SELF- CONFIDENT ATTITUDE

"I don't go by, or change my attitude, based on what people say. At the end of the day, they too are judging me from their perspective. I would rather be myself and let people accept me for what I am than be somebody who I am not, just because I want people's approval." (Karan Patel)

Belief and trust in self

This means being secure in yourself and in your position.

Secure in who you are

This is an attitude caused by having a God-given sense of security in yourself, celebrating who you are through positive self-talk and adopting a posture of self-belief.

A healthy confidence

A servant must have a healthy confidence in who they are.

"Trust yourself. Create the kind of self that you will be happy to live with all your life. Make the most of yourself by fanning the tiny, inner sparks of possibility into flames of achievement" (Golda Meir).

Secure in your competence

Do not get side-tracked by comparing yourself with others. Appreciate and celebrate the gifting, skills, and abilities of others without feeling less than them or threatened by them.

"No one can make you feel inferior without your consent" (Eleanor Roosevelt)

Secure in your value and relevance

A secure servant is one whose identity derives from the knowledge of their value, relevance, and uniqueness.

Secure in taking responsibility

This means being secure enough to take responsibility for your choices, decisions, and actions, so that you do not develop a victim syndrome or a blame-shifting attitude.

Secure in your purpose

Self-confidence means knowing your purpose and calling, your place and position, thereby serving confidently, assured that you are in your element.

"Be sure about what you want and be sure about yourself. Fashion is not just beauty; it's about good attitude. You have to believe in yourself and be strong" (Adriana Lima).

Thought Provoking Questions for Discussion

1. Do you have a long-suffering attitude in your servanthood? If not, what hinders you from having it and what are the ways you can develop a long-suffering attitude?

2. Do you have an excellent attitude in your servanthood? If not, what hinders you from having it and what are the ways you can develop an excellent attitude?

3. Do you have a diplomatic attitude in your servanthood? If not, what hinders you from having it and what are the ways you can develop a diplomatic attitude?

4. Do you have a team player attitude in your servanthood? If not, what hinders you from having it and what are the ways you can develop a team player attitude?

5. Do you have an others-oriented attitude in your servanthood? If not, what hinders you from having it and what are the ways you can develop an others-oriented attitude?

6. Do you have a positive attitude in your servanthood? If not, what hinders you from having it and what are the ways you can develop a positive attitude?

7. Do you have a self-confident attitude in your servanthood? If not, what hinders you from having it and what are the ways you can develop a self-confident attitude?

THE 7 ENDOWMENTS OF A SERVANT

For a servant to be able to perform their functions with the right attitudes, they must possess certain endowments. True servanthood does not only require an exemplary character, it also requires competence – a strong skill set wedded to inborn giftings and talents. God is faithful to equip those whom he sends. He endows a servant with just the right anointing and giftings for the specific purposes He has in mind for them.

As servants remain submitted to God and to their leaders, God will teach them things that education could never impart to them. In addition, by recognizing and honouring their leader, a servant receives an impartation of the same anointing and grace that God has given to their leader. This enables and empowers servants to serve effectively.

A good character on its own is not enough for effective performance. Competence and capability are essential too.

At the same time, as we shall see in a later chapter, competence without character is also a handicap. Dynamic servanthood combines exemplary character with an astute competence.

The servant's capabilities are therefore important; these are what are referred to as the seven endowments

Creative Imagination

A servant must have imagination and creativity in order to serve well. Creativity means being able to tap into the wisdom of God and come up with new and uncommon solutions and ways for executing one's tasks. This propels the leader to the next level of their vision.

Conscience

Our conscience is what God uses to speak to us about wrong and right. A good servant must have a strong conscience that leads them to choose the right, ethical, godly way over the convenient way.

The spirit of man is the candle of the Lord. (Proverbs 20:27)

Self-awareness/self-knowledge

Knowing one's strengths, weaknesses, limitations, and skills is known as self-awareness. This is essential if you are not to take on tasks outside your area of strength, because you will not be able to perform these with excellence. Self-awareness helps you to understand your optimum conditions for productivity - whether you are an early bird or a night owl, whether you thrive in a team or alone, whether you perform well under supervision or unsupervised.

Independent will

While being submitted to the vision of the leader, as a servant you must also have your own will, serving others because you have chosen to do so.

Volition/will power

Serving must always come from a place of free will. You must never feel that you are serving under compulsion.

A person's inner sense

This refers to the sense of right and wrong guiding your choices and your conduct. This inner sense helps you to understand complex ethical principles and to engage in right action.

There are at least seven endowments that an effective servant will possess:

The 7 Sevens

1. ENDOWED WITH WISDOM

What is wisdom? Wisdom is the ability to apply your knowledge, information, and skills to a situation. If knowledge is the *what*, wisdom is the *how*. This wisdom is sometimes imparted by God, sometimes from other sources, and it is crucial for your servanthood in every sphere of society.

Wisdom for the vision

You will need wisdom to interpret, execute and implement your leader's vision. At the same time, you will need wisdom to handle the temperaments and proclivities of your leader. You will need wisdom in observing and adhering to sensitive protocols, especially in maintaining the delicate boundaries of your relationship with the leader.

Wisdom for the people

You will need wisdom to handle and relate appropriately to team members and to the people around your leader.

Wisdom in relation to enemies

You will need wisdom in handling attacks and battles, learning how to defeat the enemies of your leader and their vision.

Wisdom through mentoring

To be a successful servant, you will need wisdom from mentors and coaches who already have the experience you need and have gone before you.

"Knowledge speaks, but wisdom listens" (Jimi Hendrix).

Even a fool is counted wise when he holds his peace; when he shuts his lips, he is considered perceptive. (Proverbs 17:28)

Praying for wisdom

A good servant will need to pray constantly for heavenly wisdom, remaining rooted in the Word of God in order to have a continuous overflow of wisdom.

2. ENDOWED WITH DISCERNMENT

Judging correctly

Discernment is the ability to judge well and perceive that which is not always physically visible. It is also the ability to decide between truth and error, right and wrong. It is a process of making careful distinctions in one's thinking.

Therefore, give to Your servant an understanding heart to judge Your people, that I may discern between good and evil. For who is able to judge this great people of Yours? 1 Kings 3:9

Discernment for his call

A sensitive servant will need discernment to respond to the complexities of their call effectively. This involves understanding their roles, responsibilities, their place, and position.

Discernment for the vision

In order to serve effectively, you will need discernment in understanding, interpreting, executing, and implementing the vision.

Discernment about your leader

As a servant you will need discernment to understand your leader's heartbeat, burdens, pain etc. As a discerning servant, you will also need to perceive your leader's moods and temperament so that you can serve them sensitively and effectively.

Discernment for the people

Additionally, as a servant you must be able to discern the attitudes, temperaments, motives of other team members and other people around your leader. This includes discerning any hidden motives or agendas in their supporters, sponsors, and followers.

Discernment for attacks and battles

You must be able to discern traps, ambushes, and battles, whether internal or external. This enables you to minimize the effects of attacks on your leader and to fight battles on behalf of your leader.

Discernment in choices and decisions

You must have discernment as regards decision making especially on fundamental issues concerning your leader and their vision. This way, you will be able to protect your leader from catastrophic errors of judgment.

3. **ENDOWED WITH THE ABILITY FOR INTERVENTION, INTERCEPTION, AND INTERCESSION (THE ESTHER ANOINTING)**

Esther, as a servant of her people, was enabled to intervene, intercept, and intercede to avert their destruction. Doing these three things requires that you have knowledge about the disagreements at hand and have the required resolution skills.

Furthermore, you must be aware that intervening, intercepting, and interceding will cost you and you may suffer physically, emotionally, spiritually (a "bloody nose"). You must also understand what successful intervention, interception and intercession looks like, or may look like, before you embark on your course of action. You must also first seek your leader's mind and heartbeat so that you do not act in a way that is contrary to what they want.

This endowment entails three elements:

- **Intervention**

As a servant, you intervene on behalf of your leader in disputes and disagreements. In the Old Testament, a good servant (armour-bearer) was an expert in using the sword and shield in battle against physical enemies. Likewise, a modern-day servant must be an expert in handling God's Word against the unseen enemy.

- **Interception**

This is the ability to identify and intercept any communication or person wanting to access the leader in order to harm or prejudice the leader's interests.

- **Intercession**

This means the ability to travail in prayer, to wage spiritual warfare, and to stand in the gap on behalf of your leader. True intercession requires going before God on behalf of another, yielding yourself, becoming deeply involved, paying a high price to serve, identifying with your leader, ruling over the situation with your prayers. It means to commit, endure, and travail. True intercession results in healing, mercy, victory, the breaking of captivity, releasing from debts, deliverance and escaping from the enemy, aversion of danger and exemption from judgement.

4. ENDOWED WITH A RADICAL FAITH (THE JOSHUA ANOINTING)

The gift of faith is an extraordinary and unshakable confidence in God's promises, power and presence that enables you to do great exploits and overcome adverse circumstances that would normally seem impossible to conquer. A vision from God given to a leader is often so vast that it is beyond both the leader and the servant in their own strength. Great visions therefore require great faith. A true servant will accordingly need the gift of faith if they are to overcome obstacles and be a source of encouragement and strength to their leader. A dutiful servant cannot afford to lose hope or faith, nor can they afford to fall into discouragement. A faithless servant who demonstrates fear, negative attitudes and pessimistic views before their leader is a great liability.

In order to maintain a strong faith, a resilient servant will surround themselves with like-minded people with a radical gift of faith. They will avoid negative, faithless people. They will be like Joshua, who surrounded himself with Caleb and avoided the ten other spies.

Having a radical faith means you will make the right positive confessions and back them with right action to demonstrate that your words align with your actions.

Having a radical faith does not deny facts or reality, it just chooses to trust that the outcome will be positive in the end. Radical faith will automatically be activated and increased because of the challenges, trials, and hardships that a servant will encounter. Faith becomes dormant in the absence of adversity. A servant should accordingly welcome and confront challenges instead of running away from them.

5. ENDOWED WITH A PROACTIVE ATTITUDE (THE JOSEPH ANOINTING)

Taking initiative

This is the ability to make things happen by taking the initiative, instead of waiting for things to happen to you. Proactive is the opposite of reactive.

Preventative control

This is the ability to prepare for or control a situation (especially a difficult or negative situation) in order to alert your leader and prevent a negative occurrence. A proactive servant will save their leader from many ugly situations.

Solution provider

In conjunction with proactivity, you need the ability to find practical solutions to difficult situations and problems, thereby becoming a burden-lifter for your leader.

Positive results

The word "proactive" has two words 'pro' and 'active', signifying that your actions must be positive and yield the desired good result.

Confront challenges

A servant who is proactive will speed up their self-development by confronting challenges head on and seeking solutions where there seem to be none.

Measured zeal

A caution, however: very proactive people may often overstep their mandates and the scope of their authority if they do not constantly heed their leader's instructions. Knowing the leader's heartbeat is crucial. Accountability is vital.

Decision making skills

A servant who is proactive is also excellent in decision making which is an invaluable asset to their leader.

6. ENDOWED WITH CREATIVITY

"You can't use up creativity. The more you use the more you have" *(Maya Angelou).*

Creativity is the process whereby something new and valuable is formed through expertise - a well-developed base of knowledge. Imaginative thinking skills provide the ability to see things in novel ways, to recognize patterns, and to make connections. An adventurous personality seeks new experiences, tolerates ambiguity and risk, and perseveres in overcoming obstacles. A creative environment sparks, supports, and refines creative ideas. Creativity doesn't wait for that perfect moment. It fashions its own perfect moments out of ordinary ones (Bruce Garrabrandt). Creativity involves inventing, experimenting, growing, taking risks, breaking rules, making mistakes, and having fun.

7. ENDOWED WITH FOLLOWERSHIP (ELISHA AND RUTH ANOINTING)

"Followership, like leadership, is a role and not a destination." *(Michael McKinney).*

A true servant is a follower and a clinger to their leader or boss. He or she is someone who is completely sold out to the vision bearer, so much so that the servant has the grace to follow and serve the leader to the ends of the earth, even when the leader becomes temperamental and tries to push you away.

Therefore, "followers are more important to leaders than leaders are to followers" (Barbara Kellerman).

The world needs more followers than leaders. Followers provide valuable support; they listen, reflect, comply with, and legitimize the leader. A wise servant establishes in their heart that they are not the leader. As the one following rather than leading, they believe a leader has a vision and a cause that are worth supporting. They believe that the leader themselves are worth following and supporting. Followership is accordingly a grace endowed upon a person who follows a leader out of free choice. We see this in Ruth's response to Naomi, Elisha's to Elijah. This kind of voluntary following is a sign of greatness not only in the one being followed, but in the one following.

True followership is a function of the heart because it is possible to follow physically but not authentically. When our hearts are not in it, then this is fake followership. Followership has great rewards (see chapter 7). The distressed debtors who chose to follow David through the wilderness for years end up in the palace with David as his mighty men. They enjoy key leadership positions. Ruth received her Boaz, plus land and children, because she followed Naomi. Elisha received a double portion of Elijah's anointing for the same reason.

A servant who is a follower can see the future greatness and potential of their leader. They do not focus on the leader's current status. The distressed debtors who followed David chose to follow him when he was a nobody in the wilderness because they saw his future greatness.

Followership requires that you trust and obey your leader even when sometimes you cannot see the whole picture or understand how things will end. This means you must exercise faith because faith is believing in what is not yet visible. Servants follow leaders "with a sense of hope and faith in their abilities and potential" (Reverend Paul Beedle).

Thought Provoking Questions for Discussion

1. What factors do you think would increase your wisdom as you serve?

2. What factors do you think would increase your discernment as you serve?

3. What factors do you think would increase your ability to intervene, intercept and intercede as you serve?

4. What factors do you think would increase your radical faith as you serve?

5. What factors do you think would increase your proactivity as you serve?

6. What factors do you think would increase your creativity as you serve?

7. What factors do you think would increase your followership as you serve?

Chapter 4

THE PLACE OF YOUR SERVANTHOOD

Locating Your Sphere, Sector and Position of Servanthood

"Be sure you put your foot in the right place, then stand firm." ~ (Abraham Lincoln)

Chapter Outline

7 Spheres of Influence in Your Servanthood

1. Politics And Governance
2. Business And Economy
3. Media
4. Arts And Entertainment
5. Education
6. Family
7. Church

7 Signposts To Locating Your Place

1. Your Place Has Traditions and Customs
2. Your Place will have Strongholds for You to Uproot
3. Your Place will have an Old Boys Club
4. Your Place Will Have Mountain Peaks for You to Scale
5. Your Place Will Have Your Footprints
6. Your Place Will Have a Celebrating Not a Tolerating
7. Your Place Will Have a Problem and a Dilemma for You to Solve

The 7 Logistical Positionings at Your Place

1. Physically
2. Mentally
3. Emotionally
4. Socially
5. Intellectually
6. Recreationally
7. Financially

INTRODUCTION

The call to serve comes with a place in which to serve. Every servant is given a location in which they are ordained to exert the greatest positive influence and impact. Each servant has a specific place where they will be planted in order to fulfil their purpose and call. That being the case, you must understand the characteristics, culture and protocol of your place and align yourself accordingly.

Your purpose is inevitably tied to a place in which you will find your identity and belonging. When you arrive at and discover your place, your gifting, talents and skills will be activated for optimum servanthood without stress or struggle. At your place, there will be a special grace upon you to thrive, excel and blossom and to be at your best (Jeremiah 1:4-19).

Furthermore, your place contains your provision. Once you locate the context of your servanthood, even those gifts that may have waned and become dormant are revived just simply by virtue of you being in your ordained place. It is because you have found your place that you will also find grace, favour and enabling.

At your place, you will also find a midwife to guide you, a people to work with and a people to serve.

In all of this, a wise servant must guard against two common errors: operating in the wrong place and the wrong position and overstepping the boundaries and mandates of their place and position. They must remain rightly planted in their place and position.

THE 7 SPHERES OF INFLUENCE IN YOUR SERVANTHOOD

The seven spheres of influence are also often referred to as the seven pillars, mountains and gateways and are believed to be the main shapers of culture in any society or nation. These culture-shaping spheres are Arts and Entertainment, Business and Economy, Church and Social Servanthood, Media, Education, Politics and Governance, and finally the Family.

Within these broad spheres of influence are sub-spheres or sub-sectors. While it is possible for someone to serve successfully in more than one sphere, most people are called to operate in what we might call a primary sphere.

The principles of serving in any of these spheres may be similar, but the skills and competencies, strategies and challenges may differ. Each sphere has its own unique functions for the empowerment of the persons within that sphere. Each has its own characteristics and peculiarities and you must understand how these affect your servanthood. Each possesses its own dynamics and politics which you must outmanoeuvre and outsmart. Each exhibits its own culture which you must understand and sieve carefully, discerning which parts you will adopt and which you will reject.

The first step is for a wise servant to locate which is the sphere in which they have been specially gifted, endowed, and skilled to serve. The second step is for the servant to position themselves securely in that sphere and in that context to become the best version of themselves with the best expression of their servanthood, allowing their giftings, talents and skills to become activated to the maximum.

While you are a servant called to serve in this sphere, and while you are equipped, gifted and endowed for this context, the truth is that you will nonetheless face fierce and vicious opposition from other persons in this arena. These people have either knowingly embraced the negative forces operating in this sphere or are innocent victims of those toxic and oppressive forces. As stated earlier, every weapon that a servant will need to fight their giants will already exist either internally within themselves as gifts or endowments, or they will be found as external resources at their place of servanthood.

Your task is to identify and locate the broader outer place, namely the sphere (area, sector, or industry) within your society and nation that you are designed and ordained to influence. In every society and nation, there are seven spheres or pillars. These are sometimes referred to as "mountains" that you were born to scale, conquer and command with positive influence. These seven spheres of culture include Politics and Governance, Education, Media, Business and Economy, Arts and Entertainment, Family and Church.

Within each of these broad spheres, there are sub-sectors. Every servant must locate their sphere or mountain of influence in order to fulfil their purpose.

"When the Lord your God brings you into the land which you go to possess, and has cast out many nations before you, the Hittites and the Girgashites and the Amorites and the Canaanites and the Perizzites and Hivites and the Jebusites, seven nations greater and mightier than you." (Deuteronomy 7:1)

The 7 Sevens

1. THE SPHERE OF POLITICS AND GOVERNANCE

"Governance is a way of organizing, amplifying and constraining power." (Rebecca MacKinnon)

Let everyone be subject to the governing authorities, for there is no authority except that which God has established. The authorities that exist have been established by God. (Romans 13:1)

Definition and Description of this Sphere

Politics (the root word in Greek means "affairs of the city") refers to a set of activities associated with the structural oversight of a country or an area. It involves making decisions that affect the region in question. Politics, to work, requires people of influence to attain and exercise positions of governance – governance understood as the organized control over a human community, particularly a state. The word governance denotes all the processes of governing, whether these systems are developed and employed by the government of a state, by a market or by a network. These processes are used within every social system: family, tribe, formal or informal organizations, a territory or across territories. They are implemented through the laws, traditions, customs, power structures and even through the language used within each of these social systems.

Governance relates to the processes of interaction and decision-making that takes place within the leadership of a group when there is a collective problem to resolve. This leads to the creation, reinforcement, or reproduction of social norms and institutions. In lay terms, governance is made up of the political processes that exist in and between formal institutions. It is through such political institutions that societies and nations are regulated.

For the one in authority is God's servant for your good. But if you do wrong, be afraid, for rulers do not bear the sword for not reason. They are God's servants, agents of wrath to bring punishment on the wrongdoers. (Romans 13:4)

Biblically speaking, when we seek to serve and influence a mountain of culture, we encounter Hittites, a word which signifies the feeling of terror and the consequent depletion of strength. Every mountain has its own giants, and these often take the form of oppression and subjugation. Your most powerful weapon in defeating them is the exercise of servanthood leadership. This is why you must pray for your leaders in every sphere.

I urge, then, first of all, that petitions, prayers, intercession and thanksgiving be made for all people, for kings and all those in authority, that we may live peaceful and quiet lives in all godliness and holiness. (I Timothy 2:1-2)

Within the sphere of Politics and Governance, many of the servant roles are ones to do with public services such as serving in the courts, energy suppliers, education, emergency services, environmental protection, health care, the military and public transport. Those called to serve in government itself will usually be leaders and their advisors, legislators, senators, members of parliament, the executive which includes the presidency, the judiciary and security forces, mayors, governors and so forth. The competencies for these will be writing and research skills, public speaking and presentation skills, expertise in social and mass media, the ability to read the room and understand your audience, crisis management and problem solving.

What are the most common giants that you will have to encounter, confront and slay in the Politics and Governance sphere of society?

The Giant of Oppression and Dictatorship

The greed for power and control and the exercise of uncontrolled selfish ambition leads often to an obsession with titles and positions, manipulation, and sabotages, and these in turn can often lead to dictatorship and the oppression of the masses through unrighteous social systems and processes. A dictatorship regime is an authoritarian form of government characterized by a single leader or group of leaders with either no party or a very weak party, one in which the people are not given an opportunity to express themselves freely and their individual rights are suppressed, leading to the abuse of their human rights. A regime that oppresses its people subjects them to harsh and cruel treatment, restraining them unjustly so that they become physically, emotionally, and mentally burdened by troubles, adverse conditions, anxiety and so forth. In some regimes, women are the primary victims of oppression; in others, it is the marginalized. *"With proper governance, life will improve for all"* (Benigno Aquino III). The most effective weapons for slaying the giant of oppression and dictatorship include the following:

1) The spirit of servant leadership which requires humility and meekness, and not being self-oriented.

2) The adoption of ethical political values and the defence of them irrespective of any circumstances. As it says in Deuteronomy 17:18-19, "When he takes the throne of his kingdom, he is to write for himself on a scroll a copy of this law, taken from that of the Levitical priests. It is to be with him, and he is to read it all the days of his life so that he may learn to revere the Lord his God and follow carefully all the words of this law and these decrees."

3) The courage of people in a society or a nation who will protest sacrificially and vocally in resistance to a dictatorship and who will mobilize others to stand up for their rights and beliefs.

The Giant of Corruption

This giant appears when human beings in leadership positions are motivated by a desire to control systems and structures for their own personal ends and selfish motives. Lack of self-control in the context of the idols of money, sex and power is disastrous.

Psalm 33:12 says, ***"Blessed is the nation whose God is the Lord, the people he chose for his inheritance."***

Corruption entails dishonest or fraudulent conduct by those in power, typically involving bribery. It involves unscrupulous, deceitful dealings and duplicity. Corruption destroys the people's trust, increases poverty by denying the weak access to what is rightfully theirs, and it threatens sustainable economic development and the promotion of ethical values and justice. Corruption destabilizes a society and endangers the rule of law.

The most effective weapons for slaying the Giant of corruption include the following:

1) *A sincere burden and zeal for the justice and welfare of the people.*
2) *Sincere servanthood motivated by a genuine others-oriented attitude and selfless actions.*
3) *Imposing heavy sanctions and penalties for those caught in corrupt dealings. This includes breaking the cycle of impunity*
4) *Empowering the people by granting them more access and participation in governance.*
5) *Strengthening the demands of the people for anticorruption measures and for servant leadership.*
6) *Enabling them to hold their leaders accountable so as to build mutual trust between their people and their leaders.*

Righteousness exalts a nation, but sin is a reproach to any people. (Proverbs 14:34)

2. THE SPHERE OF ECONOMY AND BUSINESS

Definition and Description of this Sphere

"If you don't drive your business, you will be driven out of business" (B. C. Forbes).

The function of this sphere is to provide and release resources to a state, society or other social system and in the process to model the wise stewardship of those resources, leading to fruitful productivity for all.

"The Lord God took the man and put him in the Garden of Eden to work it and take care of it" (Genesis 2:15).

The Biblical tribe that occupies this sphere of business and economy are the Canaanites, a word that denotes merchants or traffickers.

The main giant on this mountain is greed for Mammon (money) and your most powerful weapon will be surrendered and generous giving and philanthropy.

Business is the activity of making one's living or making money by producing, buying, and selling products. Simply put, it is "any activity or enterprise entered into for profit. This does not always happen through a company, a corporation, partnership, or formal organization. Business is a spectrum ranging from the street peddler to a huge corporation like Amazon.

"A business like an automobile, has to be driven, in order to get results" (B. C. Forbes)

Economy (from a Greek word signifying the management of one's household) is defined as "a social domain that emphasize the practices, discourses, and material expressions associated with the production, use, and management of resources." When the economy is functioning as it should, resources are used efficiently; there is a proper balance between the production of resources and their consumption.

"For even when we were with you, we gave you this rule: 'The one who is unwilling to work shall not eat" (2 Thessalonians 3:10).

What kinds of servanthood are required in this sphere? And what kind of competencies do such servants need to have? The types of servanthood required in this sphere include financial services, banking, accounting, entrepreneurship, business skills, management skills, the art of deal making, trading, handling stocks and shares, data mining/analytics, cross-cultural competency and communications, manufacturing, marketing, design, IT, cyber security, resource management, stewardship, and so forth.

The main giants you will have to confront and slay, and the weapons you will be required to use, are the following:

The Giant of Greed for Mammon/Materialism

This giant is the excessive love or desire for money or any possession. When this is taken to the point of being obsessed and enslaved by money and possessions, it leads to compromising one's values and ethics.

Greed arises from an inability to master money and material things and a reversal of the healthy and God-ordained order of things. Instead of being the master of money, someone becomes its slave. This giant needs to be slain because it arises from the Babylonian spirit, which is a spirit in *The Book of Revelation* associated with cruel domination and unbridled avarice. When this giant roams on this mountain, it leads to bad stewardship in finances and resources, and to extreme ruthlessness in dealing with people.

The most effective weapons for slaying the Giant of greed for mammon/materialism include the following:

1) Being devoid of and cleansed from the love of money
2) Adopting a generous, giving spirit and a strong sense of stewardship
3) Developing compassion for other people because generosity starts with compassion
4) Practising selflessness and an others-oriented attitude
5) Focusing your mind on things that are more valuable than money and possessions, like God, relationships, family etc.
6) Creating a greater purpose to pursue, one in which you resist living for yourself and resolve instead to make a positive impact on the lives of other people, realizing that you could be the answer and solution to someone else's need and problem.

The Giant of Unfair Trade Practices

This giant is manifested in the use of unfair practices of trade and unjust principles of handling and dealing with money and resources, either out of a lack of proper skills or out of outright thieving and robbery (The Gehazi spirit). It also entails unethical dealings, breaches of contracts and agreements, and in applying unfair scales and overcharging. Offering substandard goods at inflated prices and misrepresenting the quality and the standard of goods (for example, because their sell-by date has expired) are other manifestations.

The most effective weapons for slaying the giant of unfair trade practices include the following:

I.   Adopting excellent money management skills
II. Resource management (the Cyrus anointing, the Joseph anointing)
III. Setting a personal code of ethics on how you will handle and manage money and resources to resist the temptation to adopt crooked principles and ethics.
IV. Putting in place severe penalties and consequences for those breaching the rules as a deterrent to others.

The Giant of Exploitation

This is evidenced in the practice of monopolization - where someone seeks to monopolize a sector of trade of business to the exclusion of all others for purely selfish gains. This is an example of the Laban spirit, which oppresses, manipulates, hinders, and denies others from benefiting from their labour. Exploitation involves taking advantage of other people's desperation for selfish gain. It manifests in many different forms: sexual, financial, workplace, domestic servitude, marital and others. "The rich rule over the poor, and the borrower is slave to the lender" (Proverbs 22:7).

The most effective weapons for slaying the Giant of exploitation include:

1) Becoming others-oriented not self-focused
2) Having a genuine and sincere concern for the welfare of others
3) Sharing the market fairly and justly
4) Being devoid of the poverty and scarcity mentality.

"Successful people do what unsuccessful people are not willing to do. Don't wish it were easier; wish you were better" (Jim Rohn).

3. THE SPHERE OF MEDIA

"Finally, brothers and sisters, whatever is true, whatever is noble, whatever is right, whatever is pure, whatever is lovely, whatever is admirable if anything is excellent or praiseworthy think about such things." (Philippians 4:8)

Definition and Description of this Sphere

The function of this sphere is mainly to provide and transfer information and wisdom, create awareness and generally educate and empower the masses. "The great thing about social media was how it gave a voice to voiceless people" (Jon Ronson).

"The media's the most powerful entity on earth. They have the power to make the innocent guilty and to make the guilty innocent, and that's power. Because they control the minds of the masses" (Malcom X).

The term "medium" (the singular form of "media") is defined as "one of the means or channels of general communication, information, or entertainment in society, such as newspapers, radio, or television. The mass media is a diversified collection of media technologies that reach a large audience via mass communication.

The technologies through which this communication takes place include a variety of outlets.

Media is the communication outlets or tools used to store and deliver information or data. It is associated with the mass media communication businesses and is exemplified by such things as print media, the press, photography, advertising, cinema, broadcasting (radio and television), and publishing. The media also refers to news outlets that report and establish the news, TV stations and networks, web sites, radio stations and magazines.

The Biblical tribe that occupies this mountain is the Amorites, a word which denotes publicizing or announcing. The main giant here is propaganda and negative reports. Your most powerful weapon is the truth.

"Whoever controls the media, controls the mind" (Jim Morrison).

The types of competencies needed, are

- Content Provision for digital and print media.
- Managing and packaging of content
- Directing and producing show, news, programmes etc.
- Promotional advertising and marketing

The kinds of servanthood required are TV anchors, journalists, radio presenters, researchers, media owners, managers and policy makers, authors and writers, producers, and directors. Such servants need to be passionate for truth and justice, knowledgeable in world affairs, good curators of information, with excellent abilities in the following:

- Communication
- Content Management
- Marketing
- Computer technology

The main giants in this sphere are:

The Giant of Propaganda

Propaganda is information that is not objective, and which is used primarily to influence an audience and further an agenda. It often presents facts selectively to encourage a certain perception. It involves using loaded language to produce an emotional rather than a rational response to the information presented.

"The tongue has the power of life and death, and those who love it will eat its fruit" (Proverbs 18:21).

Propaganda is often associated with material prepared by governments, activist groups, companies, religious organizations, and the media itself. This giant promotes lies leading to fear and terror. It ruins reputations and careers, seriously prejudicing the welfare of the targeted individual or organization.

The most effective weapons for slaying the giant of propaganda include the following:

1) Disseminating objective information that is not biased and designed in a way to raise emotions
2) Broadcasting information in a fair and just way
3) Ensuring that there is media regulation with codes of conduct to be adhered to by all sections of the media
4) Imposing heavy penalties and consequences for breaching these codes as a deterrent to others.

The Giant of Error and Misrepresentation

This is a milder form of propaganda. Here facts are either ignored or distorted, not because of some prior agenda, but because of poor research. If the giant of propaganda is the result of corruption, the giant of error and misrepresentation is born from incompetence.

Even so, the outcome may end up being the same as propaganda. *"The soothing tongue is a tree of life, but a perverse tongue crushes the spirit"* (Proverbs 15:4). The results can include reputational destruction through broadcasting scandals. This giant operates through ignorance of facts and circumstances, incompetence, lack of skills, carelessness, and negligence.

The most effective weapons for slaying this giant are the following:

1) Researching facts and producing rigorous data
2) Broadcasting truth based on the above
3) Vetting destabilizing or libellous information before its broadcast
4) Creating strong legislation to deter the spread of misinformation
5) Imposing heavy penalties on those whose reporting is careless

The words of the reckless pierce like swords, but the tongue of the wise brings healing. (Proverbs 12:18)

The truthful lip shall be established forever but a lying tongue is but for a moment. (Proverbs 12:19)

He who speaks truth declares righteousness but a false witness, deceit. (Proverbs 12:17)

4. THE SPHERE OF ARTS & ENTERTAINMENT

He [God] has filled them with skill to do all kinds of work as engravers, designers, embroiderers in blue, purple and scarlet yarn and fine linen, and weavers all of them skilled workers and designers. (Exodus 35:35)

"The arts are a celebration of life" (Michael Douglas).

Hence, this sphere is also referred to as the sphere of celebration. It is intended to strengthen hope in people. It builds communities to speak to the heart of their culture. It champions and expresses truths that touch the senses, inform the mind, and engage the emotions.

The Arts refers to the theory and physical expression of creativity found in human societies and cultures. Major constituents of the arts include literature (including drama, poetry, and prose), performing arts (among them dance, music, and theatre - Genesis 4:21), and the visual arts (including drawing, painting, filmmaking, architecture, ceramics, sculpting, and photography).

Entertainment is a form of activity that holds the attention and interest of an audience, giving pleasure and delight.

The Biblical tribe occupying this mountain is the Girgashites, a word which means stone throwing. The main giant here is self-exaltation, lust and pride and your most powerful weapons are humility and holiness.

Then the Lord said to Moses, "See, I have chosen Bezalel son of Uri, the son of Hur, of the tribe of Judah, and I have filled him with the Spirit of God, with wisdom, with understanding, with knowledge and with all kinds of skills to make artistic designs for work in gold, silver and bronze." (Exodus 31:1-4)

The types of service offered in this sphere include providing original paintings and mixed media art, fine art photography, open-edition reproduction prints (posters), social media artwork, advertisements, the production of print/digital advertisements across platforms, and creative design (graphic design, video editing etc.). People serving in this sphere include gospel artists, fashion designers, sports people, secular singers, actors and actresses, poets and musicians, artists, sculptors, painters etc. The competencies this people in this sphere must possess include creative and artistic gifts and skills, technological skills, graphic skills, fashion skills, writing and speaking skills.

The main giants that a servant in this sphere will have to confront and slay, and the weapons required, are the following.

The Counterfeiting Giant of Perversion

To counterfeit means to imitate something authentic, with the intent of stealing, destroying, distorting, or replacing the original, usually as an illegal transaction, or otherwise to deceive individuals into believing that the fake is of equal or greater value than the real thing. Counterfeit products are fakes or unauthorized replicas. They are often produced because of the superior value of the imitated product. The word counterfeit frequently describes both the forgeries of currency and documents, as well as the imitations of items.

Perversion is a type of human behaviour that deviates from that which is understood to be orthodox or normal. Although the term can refer to a variety of forms of deviation, it is most often used to describe sexual behaviours considered abnormal, repulsive, or obsessive.

This giant seeks to produce imitations of original works in order to pervert the minds of those who consume them. The most effective weapons for slaying this giant are the following:

1) Maintaining authenticity and valuing genuine and pure creativity
2) Insisting on top quality products, rejecting any substandard mediocre goods

3) Remembering the purpose for the gift or skill and using it for that right purpose without deviation.

Whatever the spirit from God came on Saul, David would take up his lyre and play. Then relief would come to Saul; he would feel better, and the evil spirit would leave him. (1Samuel 16:14-23)

The Giant of Seduction (also known as the Celebrity Syndrome)

This giant thrives on lust, excessiveness, and licentiousness (including pride and self-glorification). It includes a sense of entitlement, extreme independence, and self-reliance and it is driven by a craving for success, fame, and money.

Those who succumb to this giant's power begin to believe that everything is about them and that they do not need God or anybody else, nor do they owe anyone for the gifts and skills that they possess.

The most effective weapons for slaying this giant include the following:

a) Being selfless and others-oriented, as opposed to being self-oriented and self-absorbed
b) Having a spirit of genuine and true servanthood with humility and submission
c) Remaining extremely grateful to God for giving you the gifts, talents and skills
d) Being likewise grateful to those who have helped you get to where you are.

5. THE SPHERE OF EDUCATION

"Education is the most powerful weapon which you can use to change the world" (Nelson Mandela).

"An investment in knowledge pays the best interest." *(Benjamin Franklin)*

Wisdom is a shelter, as money is a shelter, but the advantage of knowledge is this, wisdom preserves those who have it. (Ecclesiastes 7:12)

Definitions and Description of This Sphere

Education is the process of facilitating learning, or the acquisition of knowledge, skills, values, beliefs, and habits for positive transformation. Education takes place under the guidance of educators although learners may also educate themselves. This sphere is the area where knowledge and skills are developed by a learning process in learning institutions that employ many levels in a myriad of disciplines and curriculums. The Biblical tribe occupying this mountain are the Jebusites, a word which means threshing floor.

The main giants here are intellectualism, humanism, and arrogance. Your most powerful weapon is God's Word.

To those four young men God gave knowledge and understanding of all kinds of literature and learning. (Daniel 1:17)

The kind of service we see in this sphere tend to revolve around vocational, counselling, administrative, educational theory, special needs expertise, kindergarten care, middle and secondary school teaching skills. Servants in this sphere include teachers, tutors, coaches, mentors, counsellors, owners of learning institutions, managers of learning institutions, commission members mandated to regulate education centres, and so on. It also includes those who write the books, manual and teaching curriculums using in the classroom, and labour union members. We should also not forget those who keep schools clean and who provide food for children.

The people serving in this sphere must possess an inherent belief that a human being is not all-knowing, and they must want to impart in others the ability to acquire and apply knowledge, information, and wisdom. Additional requirements include patience, adaptability, imagination, teamwork, communication skills, leadership, and the ability to empower others to go further than yourself.

The main giants in this sphere and the weapons required are:

The Giant of Extreme Intellectualism

Intellectualism involves being obsessed with the pursuit of knowledge and complex ideas for no other reason than to promote your status and self-esteem. It involves idolising rationalism and downplaying the use of emotion and instinct in the learning process. This leads to an over-valuation of theoretical, clinical, cold, and abstract knowledge. The negative aspects of intellectualism include snobbery and arrogance, pride in one's heart, and the display of head knowledge without practical wisdom. Intellectualism is a form of idolatry in which people end up worshiping human knowledge instead of God. This simply fuels the secular mind-set of self-sufficiency.

The most effective weapons for slaying this giant include the following:

1) Having godly wisdom about how to apply acquired knowledge
2) Being able to accommodate and respect other people's views and weigh them against your own objectively and respectfully
3) Emphasizing the importance of relying on each other's contributions when making decisions, especially those that concern the lives of other people.

The Giant of Secular Humanism

This is an ungodly philosophy that glorifies humanly constructed values and qualities. It is the product of a reliance on the human intellect. It is often forged in direct opposition to God and His Word and, as such, lacks real wisdom and a workable morality. Secular humanists have a rationalist outlook, philosophy, and worldview. They attach prime importance to human rather than divine or supernatural sources of truth. As such, this giant promotes the lie that human sources of wisdom have rendered God's Word and wisdom redundant. It rejects everything divine and advocates atheism. Humanism is basically the belief that the person creates their own set of ethics without being accountable to anyone.

This philosophy has been indoctrinated into young minds for many years, resulting in dangerous beliefs. Humanism tolerates the education or teaching of almost anything and everything except Christian belief. Its rationalistic adherents argue that religious beliefs should not be practiced in a publicly funded system like a school.

The effective weapons for slaying this giant are the following:

a) Adopting and emphasizing the importance, wisdom, and indispensability of what is divine (i.e., what emanates from God's Word)

b) Submitting all human knowledge and intellect to the superior and timeless truths of God's Word

c) Practicing Godly kingdom values in this sphere of influence as an alternative, showing that the humanistic mantra of "living your own truth" is only healthy when this means living according to God's truth

d) Establishing more learning institutions designed to align people to the teachings of God in ways that are healthy and joyful

e) Infiltrating all levels and aspects of the educational sphere and overriding the ephemeral half-truths of humanistic philosophy with the eternal true truths of God's Word.

6. THE SPHERE OF FAMILY

"Family life contributes immensely to an individual's happiness. Only in a happy home life can complete contentment be found" *(Dorothea S. Koppliln).*

Anyone who does not provide for their relatives and especially for their own household, has denied the faith and is worse than unbelievers. **(1 Timothy 5:8)**

Definition and Description of this Sphere

The function of the family is to provide every human being with a sense of history (where I am from), identity (who I am and where I belong) and destiny (where I am heading). The family is the God-ordained context where human beings discover and experience the two most important needs in life – the need to belong and the need to be loved and to love.

The family is the God-ordained bedrock of a healthy society. This is where generations are birthed, where legacies are passed on. It is a group of people related either by consanguinity (by blood), affinity (marriage or other relationship), or co-residence (living together). Family comprises parents and children. It is the context where not only attachment is strengthened but where a sense of right and wrong is nurtured (morality). Thus, there is a direct relationship/connection between family and social order.

The servants in this sphere are fathers, father figures, mothers, mother figures, children, siblings, aunts, uncles, grandparents, and so on. Whether the family is nuclear, extended, or blended, everyone is a servant in this sphere. This includes house servants, cooks, nannies, gardeners, tutors, etc. In wealthier homes, it can also involve drivers, security personnel and bodyguards. Family doctors, family lawyers, family counsellors and family therapists also serve in this sphere, as do personal financial advisors, pastors, psychologists, marriage counsellors, child psychologists, and mediators. All these need the requisite skills for this sphere, including empathetic listening and emotional intelligence.

Do you see how many people serve in this sphere? There is a reason for this. "The most important thing in the world is family and love" (John Wooden).

"In family life, love is the oil that eases friction, the cement that binds closer together, and the music that brings harmony" **(Friedrich Nietzsche).**

The Biblical tribe on this mountain is the Perizzites, a word that denotes belonging to a village. The main giant here is abandonment and your most powerful weapon against him is unity and love.

The main giants in this sphere and the weapons required are as follows:

The Giant of Abandonment

This results in people suffering from an orphan spirit, a loss of identity and value, and the destruction of a sense of security and self-worth. It usually manifests as a direct consequence of absentee fathers and mothers, whether this absence is physical or emotional, and it is exhibited in runaway rebellious children, a syndrome caused by deep father and mother wounds. This sense of abandonment and rejection is caused by irresponsibility, divorce, separation, premature death, sickness, emotional disengagement, abuse, and so on. When this giant starts warring against the family, there are mental health problems, suicides, learning difficulties, criminal behaviour, ill health, and so on. The legacy can be lifelong, affecting a child's career and relationships.

The most effective weapons for slaying this giant include the following:

a) Promoting skilled pre and post marital counselling
b) Advocating for hands-on parenting
c) Teaching effective parenting skills
d) Helping couples and children to understand their roles and responsibilities in families
e) Imparting effective principles for money management, given that many family breakups are a result of financial stress
f) Making God/Jesus Christ the centre of every family
g) Building a family altar where families pray together and read the Word of God.

The Giant of Abuse

Abuse is widespread, tragically, and comes in various guises within the family unit: verbal, physical, emotional, spiritual, financial, and sexual. Some abuse is caused by mental sickness, others by everyday stress and pressures. Abuse in families can be hidden over years because family members are ashamed to expose it, fearing what others will think of them.

The most effective weapons for slaying this giant include the following:

a) Offering psychological treatment and therapy
b) Providing family counselling
c) Expose abuse rather than keeping it secret (secrecy just makes the shame a whole lot worse)

d) Seeking help and intervention without fearing the opinions of others

e) Identifying and relying on support systems within the extended family network, social services, and healthy, non-abusive local churches

Serving in the sphere of the family means you are not serving one person alone, such as a leader and their vision. You are serving the most delicate ecosystem on earth – a group of people who can easily be wounded. This means that you must serve this sphere with great sensitivity. Broken attachment in childhood leaves a lifetime of toxic consequences. Nothing is more important than creating strong family units. If you have been endowed with the proper gifting, talents, and skills to serve on this mountain, it is a noble and important calling which you will need to follow with wisdom and humility.

7. THE SPHERE OF CHURCH

"The True Church can never fail. For it is based upon a rock" *(T.S. Eliot).*

"And I tell you that you are Peter, and on this rock, I will build my church, and the gates of Hades will not overcome it." **(Matthew 16:18)**

Definition and Description of this Sphere

The church is a vital sphere of influence within a society or nation. It is a community of people who adhere to and believe in the teachings of Jesus Christ. The church, both in its universal and local expressions, is commonly referred to as "the Body of Christ."

Although "church" has come to mean a building or a denomination, the original Greek word used in Matthew 16:18 (*ekklesia*) meant "a gathering or assembly." It is the basis for our word "congregation."

And that is what God designed the church to be - a group of people. The church was never meant to be a building that you go to but a community or a family that you join.

Just as a body, though one, has many parts, but all its many parts form one body, so it is with Christ. (I Corinthians 12:12)

The word *ekklesia* literally means "the called-out ones." Notice the word "out"! The purpose of the church was never to stay inside a building and sing songs. It was, right from the beginning, to be salt and light within society, to change the world, to take God's kingdom principles in the marketplace. Don't forget, 97% of church members spend most of their time outside church buildings, serving in non-church spheres of society. Only 3% are pastors or church workers. The 97% are called to promote God's kingdom principles in all the other spheres of culture. The local church exists to equip them to infiltrate these spheres with the love, the wisdom, and the power of God, bringing the reign of God (the rule of heaven) into even the most secular areas of a nation. We were never called to stay put behind closed doors. We were called, and are called, to go and make disciples of all nations. Indeed, a nation's destiny lies in the hands of the Christians within its population.

If you are a Christian, this means that your promised land is the place of your assignment. This is not necessarily in the church sphere. Your promised land is where you manifest Christ as you serve. When this is not understood, the local church is like a room full of spotlights that keep blinding each other. It is like an over-salted dish. The church must change culture and society and cure the social ills of its day. So, focus on finding your promised land outside the church. We must be filled with God's nature to deliver and serve the nations. The church must love and help people in society before seeking to help themselves. Subdue and conquer your sphere through integrity and hard work. Work is God's calling for human beings.

In this sphere, as in every other, there is a battle between light and darkness. Whatever your promised land or place, I can guarantee that you will encounter persecution. When you do, your response reveals your character. Persecution is a refining reality; it removes your selfish nature and puts God's nature at the centre of your being. Don't forget, your promised land or place of service is the perfect platform from which you can defeat evil with good. You may not be called to be a preacher in a church, but you are called to touch lives at work, to change people and to reform society. No wonder then that your promised land and place can resemble a battlefield sometimes. But for every battle there is a weapon:

a) Trusting God during problems and hardships
b) Leaning on God's wisdom and power to rule in your promised land
c) Speaking God's Word in your promised land to fight evil
d) Confronting evil powers at your promised land for the sake of your nation
e) Using God's kingdom principles to dethrone the powers of darkness
f) Combining prayer and inspired action; there is a time to pray and a time to take practical action
g) Remaining obedient to God's guidance
h) Being a solution-provider and an answer in your place (until you arrive there, people will grope around for solutions, looking for them in the wrong places)
i) Striking, like a polished arrow, at injustices and unrighteousness in your place/promised land.
j) Remembering that the health and wellbeing of your nation belongs to you.

What are the types of servanthood required in this church sphere? The people called and ordained to serve in this unique and sacred sphere, along with the competencies required, are as follows:

- Administration
- Intercession
- Mentoring
- Counselling
- Evangelizing
- Teaching
- Pastoring

- Ministry
- Ushering
- Praise and worship
- Discipleship
- Hospital visiting
- Mercy Ministry

The principal acts of service in this sphere are

Weddings

Burials

Baptisms

Confirmations

Ordinations

Those called to serve in this sphere will naturally be mature and equipped believers in |Jesus Christ:

- Apostles
- Prophets
- Evangelists
- Teachers
- Pastors
- Bishops
- Deacons
- Elders
- Armour-bearers

The gifts, talents, and skills necessary to serve in this sphere of church are:

- Faith

- Working miracles

- Encouraging and comforting

- Preaching

- Teaching

- Prophesying

- Intercession

- Words of knowledge

- Words of Wisdom

- Discernment

- The ability to divide the Word of God accurately

Other skills in this sphere include good communication, interpersonal abilities, powerful organizational prowess, exemplary leadership qualities, humility, empathy, consistency, and proactivity. These gifts, talents, and skills will need to be discipled, harnessed, and proven through a process of spiritual formation over time. This enables you use them in the right way for the right purpose.

The main giants in this sphere and the weapons required are as follows:

The Giant of Religion

"If God cared only about religious activities, then the Pharisees would have been heroes of faith" (Francis Chan). The religious spirit is a type of demonic spirit. It causes people to replace a genuine

relationship with God with religious rules, exhausting works, and empty traditions. It focuses on an outward appearance of false piety, holiness, and righteousness (as in the case of the Pharisees).

"Sometimes we emulate the Pharisees more than we imitate Christ" *(R.C. Sproul).*

"There is no pride so dangerous, so subtle and insidious as the pride of holiness" (Andrew Murray).

In Matthew 5:20, Jesus said that our righteousness must exceed that of the Pharisees. In Matthew 23:13, *he cried,* **"Woe unto you Pharisees!"** Clearly then, the religious spirit is contrary to the Holy Spirit, the Spirit of Jesus.

The religious spirit leads to pride and a harsh judgmental spirit that is often a smokescreen for hypocrisy and self-righteousness, it seeks titles and positions of honour serves to be seen and applauded, coveting the praises of man (Galatians 1:10). The most effective weapons for slaying this "Giant of Religion" are:

1) Developing and maintaining an intimate fellowship, relationship and walk with the Holy Spirit.
2) Relying on God's empowering grace and strength instead of your own.
3) Walking in humility, relying on the righteousness of God as opposed to relying on your own righteousness.
4) Possessing a sincere love for people, a passion for serving them and a desire to see their transformation without imposing judgments and criticism, choosing to see the gold and not the garbage in them

The Giant of Idolatry

Idolatry literally means the worship of an "idol." Originally it referred to the worship of a graven image. In Abrahamic religions, such as Christianity, idolatry connotes the worship of something or someone other than God as if it were God. When we worship an idol, we fix our attention and devotion on the created rather than the Creator.

Idols today include money, material things, success, fame, other people, family, power, work, and career. Idolatry is false worship that causes death and lack; it is the worship of a creature-like object as a god. Instead of being attached to the Father (which is healthy), we allow ourselves to become overly attached to a thing or a person (which is unhealthy). When this happens, we take our focus away from God and place it on another.

As a faithful servant, sometimes you can subconsciously begin to worship your leader because of the great admiration, deep loyalty and passion you have in serving them, but you must retain a right perspective so that you worship God as you serve man. We must beware of fearing man instead of fearing God, choosing to obey man instead of God.

"Sometimes in order to obey God, we must disobey Herod" (Billy Graham).

The most effective weapons for slaying the giant of idolatry" include the following:

1) Avoiding the temptation of worshiping the leader you are serving
2) Remembering that your worship is reserved only for God
3) Maintaining the Biblical balance of serving man while you worship God
4) Avoiding the temptation of giving glory to men because all glory belongs to God.

The renowned Emperor of Ethiopia Haile Selassie told his followers *"Do not worship me, I am not God. I am only a man. I worship Jesus Christ."*

Avoid the temptation of pleasing men and seeking their approval of instead of seeking God and seeking his approval (Galatians 1:10). Paul said he was not seeking the approval of men or trying to please man. His focus was always on pleasing God.

Avoid the temptation of disobeying God in a quest to obey men when a conflict arises. Peter and the other apostles declared,

"We must obey God rather than man" (Acts 5:29).

Remember, the fear of man is a snare (Proverbs 29:25).

"Obey God's laws first before considering the laws of man" (Manny Pacquiao).

The Giant of False Doctrines (doctrinal error)

This consists of compromising the truth of God. Any doctrine that does not align with right Biblical theology, rooted in the revealed Word of God, is a false doctrine. Doctrinal error breeds deception, division, disillusionment, danger, and destruction. False doctrines are characterized by deception. They often occur in the false teachings of cult leaders who make promises they cannot keep. They breed division and destruction, causing conflicts in the family.

The most effective weapons for slaying this giant are the following:

1) Testing the origin, authority, consistency, and godliness of every doctrine to determine if it is true or false (1 Peter 2:1)

2) Ensuring you stick to the pure and unadulterated Word of God.
"A good church is a Bible-centred church. Nothing is as important as this - not a large congregation, a witty pastor, or tangible experiences of the Holy Spirit" (Alistair Begg).

3) Ensuring you are part of a Bible-teaching church whose beliefs align with the Word of God

4) Questioning where any teaching is out of alignment with the Bible

5) Rejecting any instruction or counsel that contradicts the Word of God.

Thought Provoking Questions for Discussion

1) What traits and attributes in yourself confirm that you belong to the sphere of politics and governance? How do you plan to positively influence and transform it?

2) What traits and attributes in yourself confirm that you belong to the sphere of business and economy? How do you plan to positively influence and transform it?

3) What traits and attributes in yourself confirm that you belong to the sphere of media? How do you plan to positively influence and transform it?

4) What traits and attributes in yourself confirm that you belong to the sphere of arts and entertainment? How do you plan to positively influence and transform it?

5) What traits and attributes in yourself confirm that you belong to the sphere of education? How do you plan to positively influence and transform it?

6) What traits and attributes in yourself confirm that you belong to the sphere of family? How do you plan to positively influence and transform it?

7) What traits and attributes in yourself confirm that you belong to the sphere of church? How do you plan to positively influence and transform it?

THE 7 SIGNPOSTS TO LOCATING YOUR PLACE

For every one of us, there is a specific place, area, sector where we are ordained to fulfil our purposes. Your place has a problem awaiting you to solve, so you are an answer at your place, with guaranteed resources to hand. It is a place where you are valued, celebrated, victorious and remembered – not just tolerated. This may even also be a place of your greatest battles, because of the negative forces resisting your positive impact). Nonetheless, you will be equipped to slay and silence every attack from the evil one. All the weapons you need to slay the giants at your place are within you, namely your anointing and gifting, and the external weapons that are available to you your place.

Your place will have an enemy. It will contain giants and strongholds that will do everything within their power to resist and oppose you, so it is incumbent upon you to slay, dislodge and dismantle every giant in that sphere that seeks to hinder you from serving effectively. Having been called to that sphere, you have within you the weapons necessary to slay every giant in that sphere.

1. YOUR PLACE WILL HAVE CUSTOMS AND TRADITIONS

By the time you position yourself in your ordained place, you will find that there is already an established culture that is clearly identifiable with the place. This is the culture that you must access in order to determine which aspects of that culture will be conducive for the fulfilling of your purpose and which will be counter-productive to your purpose. You must then have a divine strategy of how to dismantle the negative culture and replace it with a positive culture without either creating chaos or destabilizing the place.

2. YOUR PLACE WILL HAVE STRONGHOLDS FOR YOU TO UPROOT

You are going to your ordained place to cause a positive impact, influence, and transformation. However, there will be giants in the form of opposition, obstruction and hindrances who want to keep their status quo and maintain the negative influences and activities in your sphere. You are equipped, anointed, and endowed with the right qualities to slay all those giants.

There will be at least five giants that will manifest most viciously, irrespective of the sphere of influence where you are serving:

- The giant of injustice
- The giant of immorality
- The giant of corruption
- The giant of discrimination
- The giant of oppression

Fortunately, as stated earlier, you are already equipped and endowed with five smooth stones to enable you defeat these giants:

- Supernatural wisdom
- Radical faith
- Amazing grace
- Fervent prayer
- Rigid righteousness

3. YOU PLACE WILL HAVE AN OLD BOYS CLUB

The old guard is made up of those who have taken ungodly ownership and control of your sphere and will try to thwart and rebuke you. Your purpose for going to your ordained place is to become an authority, an owner, and a voice. This means that you are not going there as a visitor. The old guard must either receive and embrace you or move out and make way for you. The old guard is usually composed of those who have failed to make the impact they thought they would make in that place. They have become irrelevant and must move out. For example, in the 1 and 2 Samuel, we find King Saul (the old guard) as God was preparing David to replace him. However, King Saul fought and resisted David viciously. That said, he did not destroy David.

At your place, you will encounter "the spear of Saul" and, like David, you will use the weapons of wisdom and righteousness to defeat it. This spear symbolizes oppression and injustice. You will not use underhandedness or fight evil with evil.

4. YOUR PLACE WILL HAVE MOUNTAIN PEAKS FOR YOU TO SCALE

The levels you need to attain are like mountain peaks that you must conquer. You are to be strategically positioned at the top of your mountain, but first you must make sure that you "peak" in the following five areas on the way there. Each one of these are milestones in your servanthood within your sphere:

- The peak of your presence
- The peak of your logistic positioning
- The peak of your relevance
- The peak of your value
- The peak of your influence.

5. YOUR PLACE WILL HAVE YOUR FOOTPRINTS

Having discovered your purpose, there will also be a seat for you on the bus. You must position yourself in your right seat because only from your right seat will you be able to strive, conquer and command. When you find it, however, you will see someone already seated there; you must dethrone them in a wise way.

Your footprints are symbolic of the impression, market effects, impacts and presence that you make at your place. To leave a lasting footprint, you must be prepared to step, press, and make a bold stand. This must be done intentionally. You must not creep around and walk light-footedly, as one who does not want to be heard, or seen, or leave any mark or presence. Leave you footprints in the place of your destiny.

6. YOUR PLACE WILL HAVE YOUR CROSS AS WELL AS YOUR CROWN

You will fight the greatest battles at your place, but you will also gain your greatest victories there. You will suffer the deepest hurts at your place, but you will also have your greatest joy there. Take heart. Once you locate and arrive at your right place and once you embark on fulfilling your purpose effectively and successfully, you will eventually become celebrated and not just tolerated. At your place, you will have a cross to bear, pain to endure, sacrifices to make and losses to incur, but it is in that same place that you will receive your crown once you have endured your cross. Your cross must come before your crown.

7. YOUR PLACE WILL HAVE A PROBLEM AND A DILEMMA FOR YOU TO SOLVE

The reason that place has been ordained for you is because you have been equipped and endowed to solve a problem there and be an answer to a dilemma. You will quickly and clearly discern the problems and dilemmas which no one else seems to see and you will have solutions, answers and strategies that no one else seems to possess.

Thought Provoking Questions for Discussion

1. Are there aspects of the culture at your place of servanthood that you deem abhorrent or against your values? If so, how did you deal with it?

2. What giants at your place have you encountered and what weapons did you use to slay them?

3. Have you encountered old guards at your place of servanthood and if so, how did you escape their spears?

4. What are the most challenging mountain peaks at your place?

5. Do you feel that you have made sufficient footprints at your place?

6. Do you feel celebrated at your place of servanthood? If so, how?

7. What kind of problems and dilemmas have you found at your place of servanthood and how did you solve them?

THE 7 LOGISTICAL POSITIONINGS AT YOUR PLACE

A wise servant will be logistically positioned as well as strategically aligned to the leader they are serving, the vision of that leader, to the people they are serving with and to the people benefiting from the vision. This positioning will be in every aspect of life as far as it is practically possible without breaching the boundaries of propriety. Positioning and alignment in this context refer to giving support to the persons and the vision that you are serving.

The 7 Sevens

1. PHYSICALLY POSITIONED AND ALIGNED

This means being physically present in terms of locality because effective service requires physical presence. It means physical proximity, in order to be available and accessible when needed. It means being physically involved in the affairs and welfare of your leader, the vision and those around you, not working by "remote control" or in the "spirit". It means being physically aligned enough to listen and hear instructions. It means being physically aligned enough to see and observe what is happening around your leader, the vision and those with whom you are serving. It means being physically aligned enough to act and take actions should the need arise. It means being physically aligned enough to learn and be mentored by your principal.

2. MENTALLY POSITIONED AND ALIGNED

This means being of one mind and in agreement on issues pertaining to the welfare of the leader, the vision and those around you, and those you are serving. It means that your mind is on the same level in terms of sharpness, alertness, and preparedness. It means that you are positive minded with the same measure of strength and stamina. It means that you all have creative minds and are all creative thinkers. It means that all have focused, stable minds with the capacity for concrete thinking, able to apply factual knowledge and showing your experience by being focused on the tasks at hand. It means being a critical thinker, insightful, able to solve problems by thinking outside the box. It means both having an open mind, able to accommodate new ideas and concepts.

3. EMOTIONALLY POSITIONED AND ALIGNED

Emotions are strong feelings caused by circumstances, relationships, moods, sentiments, instincts, intuitions and passions. Alignment in this area means that you are knit together with others in heart and soul in an affectionate bond. It means you are grieved and pained by the same things as they are and are equally passionate for similar things. It means you all have similar emotional energy, vibrancy, and enthusiasm, and that you possess similar emotional strength to handle tough times and issues.

There is such a thing as "emotional forsaking" whereby one is physically present but emotionally cut off from others. A faithful servant must be careful not to emotionally forsake their leader, or the vision, or those around that leader because this may lead to total emotional disconnection, making it difficult for you to serve effectively. Being emotionally aligned must have its boundaries and it must never lead to over familiarity or inappropriate closeness. This will erode the respect and honour a servant should have for their leader, and their passion for the vision and empathy for those with whom they are serving.

4. SOCIALLY POSITIONED AND ALIGNED

The person serving, the principal and those around him will have shared values as regards relationships. They will all be aligned as regards family values and the priority of family. They will be aligned with their views on health and wellbeing, social etiquette and social protocol, work ethics and professional etiquette. They will be aligned in terms of their social awareness. They will be aligned in their opinion of ills and dysfunctions in society.

5. INTELLECTUALLY POSITIONED AND ALIGNED

Being intellectually aligned means that a person serving their leader and those around them will all be equally hungry and thirsty for information, for understanding concepts, and for analysing data. It means all will have the ability to understand complex ideas. They will all have an ability to understand new ideas and information from a rational rather than emotional point of view. They will all have high emotional intelligence (EQ) with good people and social skills, self-awareness and so on. All will have a high IQ for purposes of keeping up with one another. They will all be cognizant of the fact that intellectualism is secondary to wisdom, so they will not over rely on their intellects and they will know when and when not to give it emphasis.

6. RECREATIONALLY POSITIONED AND ALIGNED

"People who cannot find time for recreation are obliged sooner or later to find time for illness" (John Wanamaker)

Recreational alignment refers to social interactions and activities that are beneficial for the mental, emotional, and physical wellbeing, reducing stress and developing social skills or soft skills. Recreational alignment relates to activities done for enjoyment when one is not working. These bring pleasure and relaxation. A socially aware person will take note of their leader's recreational interests and activities. They will then seek to develop similar recreational activities to promote a deeper bond between themselves and their leader. This will naturally result in more effective service. In order to relax and de-stress, everyone involved should be able to move away from the heavy responsibilities of the vision and take a breath of fresh air together in other activities.

"The bow cannot always stand bent, nor can human frailty subsist without some lawful recreation" (Miguel de Cervantes).

The best ideas and strategies often come to a leader and person serving when they are in playful mode.

"Eight hours work, eight hours sleep, and eight hours recreation - Brigham Young" (Susa Young Gates).

Sharing recreational activities will enable a person serving, as well as their leader, to know each other more and appreciate other aspects of one another. These recreational activities will bring out their soft human aspects, making them more appealing to the other people they are dealing with while fulfilling the vision.

7. FINANCIALLY POSITIONED AND ALIGNED

A servant, his leader and those around him will possess good money and resource management skills when it comes to financial matters. They will also exhibit good stewardship of resources generally. They will demonstrate honourable, ethical integrity in dealing with finances and resources, holding common, shared values. It means they will all possess a similar money language, money personality and money habits. They will all be masters of money as opposed to being mastered by money. They will all have a mentality of abundance rather than a poverty mind-set in relation to money and resources.

Since they are all serving the same vision with similar goals, objectives, and expectations, they will be aligned in their use and application of the resources available. They will be aligned in terms of their financial acumen and ability to understand money concepts.

"Money is only a tool. It will take you wherever you wish, but it will not replace you as the driver" (Ayn Rand)

Thought Provoking Questions for Discussion

1. What challenges have you encountered in strategically aligning yourself **physically** to your leader and those around you in service?

2. What challenges have you encountered in strategically aligning yourself **emotionally** to your leader and those around you in service?

3. What challenges have you encountered in strategically aligning yourself **mentally** to your leader and those around you in service?

4. What challenges have you encountered in strategically aligning yourself **recreationally** to your leader and those around you in service?

5. What challenges have you encountered in strategically aligning yourself **socially** to your leader and those around you in service?

6. What challenges have you encountered in strategically aligning yourself **intellectually** to your leader and those around you in service?

7. What challenges have you encountered in strategically aligning yourself **financially** to your leader and those around you in service?

This Page Was Intentionally Left Blank

Chapter 5

THE PEOPLE OF A TRUE SERVANTHOOD

Identifying And Relating to the People Within Your Servanthood

"Success isn't about how much money you make. It's about the difference you make in people's lives"

~ (Michelle Obama)

Chapter Outline

The 7 Types of Characters and their Nemesis in Your Servant Hood

1. An Admirer and a Mocker
2. A High Achiever and a Mediocre
3. An Ally and a Adversary
4. A Sponsor and a Saboteur
5. A Little Brother Syndrome & a Big Brother Syndrome
6. A Loyalist and a Betrayer
7. A Free Giver and a Free Loader

The 7 Codes and Terms of Engagement

1. To Build Boundaries
2. To Cut out Cliques
3. To Contain Confidentiality
4. To Honour Hierarchy
5. To Exercise Emotional Intelligence
6. To see the Gold not the Garbage
7. To Safeguard Sanctuary

The 7 Ways of Relating With Your Leader

1. Behind
2. Besides
3. Ahead
4. Above
5. Around
6. Apart
7. Within

INTRODUCTION

Your servanthood is not a solo affair; it involves relating to people. As one desiring to serve effectively, you must be cognizant of the fact that your servanthood will inevitably involve diverse relationships. Your ability to identify those relationships and your capacity to relate and respond to them appropriately will greatly determine the effectiveness of your servanthood. As a wise servant, playing your cards right in each of these relationships, even those that look like they are negative, will end up propelling you forward into more success.

"There is a story behind every person, there is a reason why they are where they are. Think about that, and respect who they are" (Marc and Angel Chernoff).

Your call to servanthood will involve three fundamental relationships that you will need to master:

1. With those you are serving, namely your leader/leadership
2. With the beneficiaries, or the section of the community, that is receiving value from the vision
3. With your co-servants and co-workers

In this chapter, we are going to examine at least seven types of characters, as well as their nemesis characters (in other words, their opposites), that you will encounter in your servanthood. We will also identify at least seven codes/terms of engagement that you will need to adhere to in order to successfully relate to those you encounter. Lastly, we will look at seven ways of positioning yourself in relation to your leader, all of which have a bearing on how effective you will be in the discharge of your servanthood role.

THE 7 TYPES OF CHARACTERS AND THEIR NEMESIS YOU WILL ENCOUNTER IN SERVANTHOOD

You must learn to identify the different characters that you will encounter in your servanthood and you will need to study their characteristics, proclivities, their motives and intentions towards you. You will need to understand how to position yourself vis-à-vis each character, understand the role and value of each character to you and your servanthood, and how to respond and relate to each one appropriately, so that the relationship enhances your servanthood rather than limiting it.

You will encounter at least seven types of characters and their nemeses: (1) the admirer and the mocker, (2) the high achiever and the mediocre achiever, (3) the ally and the adversary, (4) the sponsor and the saboteur, (5) the little brother and the big brother, (6) the loyalist and the betrayer, (7) the free giver and the freeloader.

The 7 Sevens

1. THE ADMIRER AND THE MOCKER

"There is an innocence in admiration: it occurs in one who has not yet realized that they might one day be admired." (Friedrich Wilhelm Nietzsche)

The admirer is your champion, cheerleader, soother. These characters are crucial in boosting your morale during your servanthood. The intention and motive of your admirer is to act as an enthusiastic vocal supporter who has great admiration and high regard for you, who respects, appreciates, commends and praises you.

"For me, the best thing about winning an award is when the people cheer for your win. When you can see that the people are really happy that you are winning something, that's the most rewarding thing in the world" (Busta Rhymes).

The best way to respond and relate to your admirer is by appreciating their support and encouragement and reciprocating likewise. Beware of becoming puffed up by the admiration and applause, thinking you have arrived and then settling into a comfort zone where your progress is halted.

"As athletes, we're always going to have aches and pains, but when your teammates cheer you on, you don't think about it" (Simone Biles).

The mocker is the one who causes you repeated emotional pain, distress or annoyance, heckling, taunting and ridiculing you, tormenting and belittling you. This usually comes in the form of a person who is in a better position, has more advantages and privileges than you and who sees you as a threat. The reason they seek to break you is because they know their situation is temporary and that the tables could turn any minute, placing you above them. You will encounter mockers more often in barren seasons when you feel as if you are not moving forward or upwards.

"Your mockers will only have your attention if you give them your attention" (Ernest Agyemang Yeboah).

The intention and motive of the mocker is to break you and derail and distract your focus from your main goal so that you waste your energy reacting to them instead of focusing on your servanthood. A mocker's motive is to anger you into hitting back, or to seriously discourage you to the point of giving up.

"Your mockers will only have your attention if you give them your attention" (Ernest Agyemang Yeboah).

The best way to respond to the mocker is to ignore them completely and focus solidly on your servanthood and your goals. You need to keep in mind that your mocker has absolutely nothing you require on your journey to where you are going and what you are accomplishing. The only value a mocker can add to your life is provoking and propelling you to be even more focused, passionate and zealous in pursuing your servanthood and goals, thereby improving yourself and the quality of your servanthood. This will lead you to reach an even higher level than the mocker. While the mocker is mocking, you are wisely and quietly rising above and overtaking them.

"Don't give up the fight. Don't dim out the light. Those who at first don't believe in you, will soon begin to ask you 'how did you do it?' Keep it up!" (Israelmore Ayivor).

Whether you are encountering an admirer or a mocker, it is you who determines how they affect you and your servanthood - whether they propel you to greater effectiveness or stop you from being effective.

2. THE HIGH ACHIEVER AND THE MEDIOCRE ACHIEVER

"Champions keep playing until they get it right." (Billie Jean King)

The high achiever is one who seeks to reach, attain and accomplish the intended goals with excellence, in record time and with fine self-management skills. They refuse to settle for less and aim for the highest possible level and quality of servanthood. They have a winning mentality. Formula One champion Lewis Hamilton said, *"I knew I would win. It was just a matter of time."*

The intentions and motives of a high achiever are to rise above what is expected of them, to excel and deliver above and beyond their fellow servants.

"If you want to achieve excellence, you can get there today. As of this second, quit doing less-than-excellent work" (Thomas J. Watson).

The best way to relate and respond to the high achiever is to observe, learn and emulate them by associating with them and allowing them to provoke and challenge you in your servanthood. Beware of becoming intimidated by a high achiever, thereby becoming mesmerized and paralysed into losing your confidence, believing the lie that you do not have what it takes.

"What you get by achieving your goals is not as important as what you become by achieving your goals" (Henry David Thoreau).

The mediocre achiever is unambitious and uninspired, without any drive or initiative. They are not proactive; they are lazy and lethargic, settling for less than what they are capable of or entitled to. A mediocre worker does not have a revelation regarding your call, so they do not understand why you are aiming so high. In the Old Testament, Elkana could not understand why his wife Hannah was desperately seeking to have a child when he was already providing all the material things, he thought she needed. Mediocre minds usually dismiss anything which reaches beyond their own understanding.

The intention and motive of a mediocre achiever is to dissuade you from aiming high and to persuade you to settle for less like themselves. They resent your passion and zeal and will sometimes try to circumvent your aspirational efforts by obstructing, distracting and derailing you so that you may lose focus.

The best way to respond and relate to a mediocre achiever is to avoid explaining yourself since they have no revelation about your call. You should continue with your high-achiever mentality without disclosing your plans to them and without allowing them to derail or distract you. Beware of being enticed by them into believing the lie that they are right and that you are wasting your time aiming as high as you are.

"Mediocre people don't like high achievers and high achievers don't like mediocre people" (Nick Saban).

Whether you are dealing with a high achiever or a mediocre achiever, it is up to you how they affect you and your servanthood.

3. THE ALLY AND THE ADVERSARY

The ally is a type of co-servant who identifies with you, recognises your value and understands your challenges as you serve together. They appreciate your efforts and recognise you as relevant to those you are serving and to themselves. They have a similar spirit, values and work ethics to yours.

"Be an encourager; the world already has enough critics" (David Willis).

The intention and motive of an ally is for you to excel and succeed together, to uplift you and edify you in your servanthood.

"Be encouraged to be an encourager. It's a spiritual art that everyone can learn. And mostly you learn by practicing it" (Jill Briscoe).

The best way to respond and relate to an ally is by also uplifting them, appreciating their value and relevance, sharing strategies, skills and information with them for greater effectiveness in your servanthood. Beware, however, of over-depending on an ally to the extent that if they are absent, you become ineffective. Remember, you are whole and able on your own, but even better when you are with them.

"An encourager makes habits out of envisioning success for themselves and others and teaching us to do the same" (Cathy Burnham Martin).

The adversary is one who is your opponent, competitor, rival, combatant and contender. They seek to outmanoeuvre you in your efforts. They are your enemy and the enemy of your servanthood.

"If you don't take an opponent seriously, they'll surprise you" (Canelo Alvarez).

Their motive is to destroy you and your servanthood, render you totally ineffective, attack and criticise your every effort, and engage in dubious clandestine methods of derailing you.

The best way to respond and relate to your adversary is to remain alert, sensitive and guarded against their schemes and strategies. Your best weapon against them is being empowered and increasing the value and quality of your servanthood. Beware of wasting your precious energy and time by engaging in wicked strategies against them. This will lower you to their level, making you no better than them. You outsmart your adversary by ensuring you maintain your dignity and decorum.

Whether you are dealing with an ally or adversary it is up to you to determine whether they enhance or limit your servanthood by how you respond.

4. THE SPONSOR AND THE SABOTEUR

"Sponsorship is sometimes about people behind the scenes who are sitting in rooms determining your assignments and your next career step, and you don't even know who they are" (Cathy Engelbert).

The sponsor is the type of person who will undertake the responsibility to be committed to your development and progress during your servanthood by providing you with support, whether in material form or in the form of mentorship, to help you succeed. Such a person will endorse you, back you and open doors and opportunities for you to enhance your servanthood.

The motive of a sponsors is to use their own advantages, privileges, networks and relationships, resources and experiences to help you serve at your best.

"Sponsorship is about putting your name and reputation on the line for someone else. It could be as simple as recommending someone for a new role, yet it's one of the most powerful cultural tools any organization has" (Lynne Doughtie).

The best way to respond and relate to a sponsor is to appreciate them, embrace them, to be attentive and teachable, and to harness their assistance to be the best you can be in your servanthood. A sponsor helps to keep you humble since you know that you cannot win on your own. In addition, you must remember that a day will come when you will need to be a sponsor to another. Beware of prematurely disconnecting from your sponsor by imagining that you have reached the top of your game when you have not.

The saboteur is jealous and envious of your position, zeal and passion. They resent the privileges and favour that you may be receiving from the leader and seek to undermine you. They seek to subvert you and malign you by giving false reports to your leader and to others with a view to causing disaffection. They want to make you lose face and favour in order to isolate and alienate you, thereby making your servanthood ineffective.

The best way to respond and relate to your saboteur is to walk in extreme wisdom and discernment. This will always keep you one step ahead of them without allowing them to know that you know their schemes against you. They will present as a friend to gain access to your methods of servanthood in order to sabotage them. It is therefore imperative to maintain strong and strict boundaries to yourself and your information.

Whether you are dealing with a saboteur or a sponsor, it is up to you how they affect you and your servanthood depending on your ability to respond and relate to them.

5. THE LITTLE BROTHER AND THE BIG BROTHER

The little brother is another type of person you will encounter in your servanthood. They look up to you, copy your every move, mannerism and methods and generally want to be you. The danger of the little brother syndrome is that you can end up oversharing information and yourself without any restrains. The intentions and motives of a little brother are to shadow you either to learn from you or to outshine and overtake you.

"He genuinely had my best interests and my goals for growth at heart. As a result, that mentorship changed my career path" (Lyn Immerman).

The best way to relate to a little brother figure is to first understand whether the person's motives for learning from you are genuine. If they are, be generous in allowing them to access your wisdom. If they are to present your ideas as their own, you need to guard and protect yourself. Whether you encounter this syndrome in its positive or negative aspect, you must beware not to allow it to drain your energy or derail you.

"A mentor enables a person to achieve. A hero shows what achievement looks like" (John C. Mather).

Then there is **the big brother**. This is the controller who seeks to monitor and micromanage you with a dictatorial attitude. This person is insecure, threatened by the potential and capacity they see in you. They seek to highlight your weaknesses and failings to make you feel what they feel -not good enough. The intentions and motives of a big brother are to lord it over you as one who knows better than you. They seek to control how far and how high you climb.

The best way to response and relate to people displaying this big brother syndrome is to insist that your roles and responsibilities be clearly defined. The hierarchy of authority and rank must also be clearly spelt out. You must seek to understand what relevance the person with a big brother syndrome has in your servanthood to determine the extent of your accountability to them. You could then simply ignore them, making it clear that you are not required to justify yourself to them. You could also use their criticisms to grow when you feel these maybe valid. Keep your focus on the real leader you are serving so that one with a big brother syndrome does not cause your loyalty to be divided.

When you are dealing with a little or a big brother, it is up to you how they affect you and your servanthood depending on your ability to respond and relate to them.

6. THE LOYALIST AND THE BETRAYER

The loyalist is the type of person who has your back, covers your mistakes, supports you and keeps standing up for you because they believe in you and see the value and relevance of your servanthood.

The intentions and motives of a loyalist are to defend you from those seeking to undermine, hinder and derail your servanthood, or from those seeking to take advantage of your mistakes and shortcomings.

The best way to relate and respond to a loyalist is to appreciate them and keep them close by sharing your frustrations and challenges so that they can defend you even more in the future.

The betrayer is usually a person presenting as a friend to access your personal life. They do this to know as much as possible about your methods of servanthood and the secret of your success so they can then use what they know against you.

A betrayer will butter you up, kiss you with false affection and entice you with deception to disclose confidential information about your leader and the vision. Betrayal is extremely painful because it usually comes from someone close to you and because you end up feeling guilty for having made yourself vulnerable. You extended trust to them in good faith and now that trust has been abused.

Sometimes a betrayer is more interested in destroying your leader by using you to expose your leader and the leader's vision.

"For there to be betrayal, there would have to have been trust first" (Suzanne Collins).

The best way to respond and relate to a betrayer is by becoming more guarded. You must let the betrayer know that having broken your trust it will take a long time to rebuild it, and it may never be rebuilt. Betrayal is inevitable. When it happens, you must choose to either learn valuable lessons from it and thereby become a more effective servant, or allow it to make you bitter, resentful and unable to trust again. However, the inability to trust will make you overly suspicious and paranoid, unable to have meaningful working relationships with others. This in turn will paralyze your servanthood.

"When people don't respect one another, seldom is there honesty" (Shannon L. Alder).

Whether you are dealing with a loyalist or a betrayer, it is up to you how they affect you and your servanthood depending on your ability to respond and relate to them.

7. THE FREE GIVER AND THE FREELOADER

The free giver is one who gives before taking, always giving more than they take, an others–oriented person who sincerely goes out of their way to give generously to you, whether this is in the form of material substance, time and energy, or moral support in assisting you to fulfil your servanthood. This is the person who is ready to step in and do excess duties, even duties that others despise and do not want to undertake.

A free giver's intentions and motives are for the leader, the vision and the people to succeed. A free giver seeks to support, uplift and promote others as far as possible. That being the case, you must be careful not to take unfair advantage of them, or allow others to do the same, and you must advise free givers where to draw the line between legitimate free giving and an unreasonable generosity that leaves them drained to the extent where their own servanthood is compromised.

The best way to respond and relate to a free giver is to appreciate and encourage them, to graciously accept and receive whatever help and assistance they give you in whatever form it comes.

The freeloader is the opposite: they are users, parasites, leeches, spongers, hangers-on who take much more than they give, who are supported by others without returning the favour. This person is lazy. They will happily derail and distract you from your own assignments and responsibilities, thereby seriously prejudicing your servanthood to your leader and the vision. A freeloader is one who has mastered the art of taking advantage of, and stealing the credit from, hardworking conscientious servants.

The freeloader's intentions and motives are to abuse and take advantage of your goodwill, generosity and kindness. They will burden and overwhelm you with their assignments and duties using deception and cunning to evade their own responsibilities.

The way to relate and respond to a freeloader is to master the power of saying "No!" You must resist every deception that derails you and compromises your own servanthood. You must resist anyone who seeks to deplete your time and energy for the wrong purpose. A freeloader is like a parasite or a tick that sucks the energy out of a hardworking servant, leaving them drained and ineffective.

"Light attracts light. But sometimes your light attracts moths and your warmth attracts parasites. Protect your space and energy" *(Warsan Shire).*

Whether you are dealing with a free giver or a freeloader, it is up to you how they affect you and your servanthood depending on your ability to respond and relate to them.

Thought Provoking Questions for Discussion

1. Have you ever encountered an admirer or a mocker and how did it affect your servanthood?

2. Have you ever encountered a high achiever or a mediocre achiever and how did it affect your servanthood?

3. Have you ever encountered an adversary or an ally and how did it affect your servanthood?

4. Have you ever encountered a sponsor or a saboteur and how did it affect your servanthood?

5. Have you ever encountered a little brother or a big brother and how did it affect your servanthood?

6. Have you ever encountered a loyalist or a betrayer and how did it affect your servanthood?

7. Have you ever encountered a free giver or a freeloader and how did it affect your servanthood?

THE SEVEN CODES AND TERMS OF ENGAGEMENT

"Many workplace-related problems are rooted in a communication breakdown. These can be as simple as not really hearing what the other person is saying, because we get caught up in our own fixed perspectives" (Sumesh Nair).

Anyone seeking to excel in servanthood must set up and maintain certain personal rules of conduct and terms of engagement in order to manage each of the seven relationships described in the previous section. These will enable you as a wise servant to control how you relate to each of these characters and how they will relate to you, thereby establishing a conducive and healthy working environment and atmosphere. We call these *the Seven Terms of Engagement in Your Servanthood.*

Setting, developing and maintaining crystal clear terms of engagement with the people you are serving and those you are serving with is crucial in order to avoid unnecessary chaos and conflicts.

Setting and observing a personal code of conduct will enable you as a wise servant to maintain consistency, integrity and dignity even in the most stressful and frustrating circumstances.

Your established code of conduct and terms of engagement will give you some measure of control and stability even in the most toxic working environments.

During your servanthood, you will realize that you are not the only one serving the leader and their vision. There are others serving with equal zeal. This means that a competitive atmosphere, whether negative or positive, is inevitable. As a wise servant, you must learn how to relate appropriately to your fellow servants even during fierce competition so as not to prejudice your servanthood.

Even if your co-servant and fellow team members do not set their own personal codes of conduct or terms of engagement, it is prudent for you to do so. This will guide and influence other servants positively; they will see the need to adopt a personal code of conduct for more effective co-working.

A wise person must guard against regarding their leaders and co-servants as personal friends. A wise servant must remember that these are professional relationships. Your inability to distinguish and separate your professional workplace relationships and your personal private relationships will lead to misguided expectations, and then to disappointments and frustrations.

The wise servant will learn how to build boundaries, avoid and cut out unhealthy cliques, contain and maintain confidentiality and trust, observe and honour their hierarchy and rank within the field of their servanthood, exercise high levels of emotional intelligence, respectfully see the gold and not the garbage in others, and guard their sanctuary.

"Unity, to be real, must stand the severest strain without breaking" *(Mahatma Gandhi).*

As you serve in a team there will be fundamental areas of unity that you and they will need to emphasize and action. As stated in a previous chapter, the leader or section of people you will be serving will require other people besides you to serve them so you must inevitably become part of a team. Also as stated in an earlier chapter, the vision or cause is always bigger than you and therefore will require more people than just you for it to be fulfilled successfully. Unity will accordingly become a vital value for you to adopt and master. This is referred to as the Seven Unities In Your Servanthood.

Having understood that co-servants are an inevitable component of their servanthood, an emotionally intelligent servant will understand the need for solid teamwork. They must purpose to be an integral part of their team and consciously contribute to its achievements because ultimately the team success is necessary for the leader's success. Anyone called to serve will therefore soon realize that there are others likewise called to serve a leader and their vision, albeit in different positions, capacities and roles. Each person has different gifts for the same purpose and vision.

While each servant will have their place, sphere, position and roles, together they will have to work in synergy as a team. When failures and losses come, they are all responsible and they should share the blame together.

Good co-workers must have the ability to run and win a three-legged race. They must stay tied together and run-in sync in order to win.

"Now he who plants and he who waters are one, and each one will receive his own reward according to his own labour. For we are God's fellow workers; you are God's field, you are God's building" **(I Corinthians 3:8-9).**

This entails each person surrendering part of themselves (one leg). Each must symbolically be the same height and weight – that is, one mind and spirit in agreement and in co-operation. So, whether one is planting, and another is watering, both are serving one master and one vision. Both have been entrusted with the same revelation and with the same mission. You cannot win the race without co-workers. A three-legged race is difficult because it involves leaning on one another, stumbling and falling together, failing, encouraging and picking each other up and, perhaps most important of all, a lot of laughter!

A wise servant will need to keep considering three crucial matters:

1. The different types of characters they are working with
2. The various points of unity that will be required to ensure a healthy team can work well together.
3. The personal rules and codes of conduct they will need to adopt and operate if they are to thrive and fulfil their mission and purpose.

A servant who is unable to cope and work with his fellow servants will not be effective and successful in their servanthood.

Remember, there are three different levels of unity:

Acceptance

This is the lowest level where people keep quiet without offering any opinion and hence their silence is interpreted as acquiescence. This is normally seen either where people do not care, or they are too timid or too aloof.

Agreement

The second level is where people assent in their minds but not in their hearts because they are not personally invested in the issues at hand or in the decisions being made. This is manifested in a failure to verbalize or vocalize concerns.

Alignment

The third and highest level is where people are fully committed to the leader and the cause even though they may not agree totally on every detail. This is manifested in a holistic servanthood of mind, body and heart.

It is this third level of unity that everyone in a team should aspire to because even when there may be disagreement on matters of detail, everyone is fully aligned to the vision, to their individual roles and responsibilities, and to the goal of serving effectively and successively. They do this because there is a safe atmosphere for opposing opinions. This team is where differences and diversity are welcomed in theory and respected in practice. It is a team where trust has been built over time.

"We cannot be separated in interest or divided in purpose. We stand together until the end" (Woodrow Wilson).

Alignment accordingly concerns the team's ability and capacity to be united in the desired aims, goals and objectives and the desired outcomes and expectations of the vision. This will require all the team members to have a common understanding of what the leader's vision means and entails. A good servant must seek to understand areas of the vision that they do not yet understand. Likewise, they should be sensitive and patient with others who do not yet grasp that vision to also seek understanding.

A good servant must align themselves to the unanimous decisions of the team unless they have a very valid reason to think that other team members are derailing or deviating from the vision. They must always be eager to ensure that they are of one mind and one spirit with the other team members. They will empathize with and bear the burdens of their team members. All the team members should be united and passionate in seeing the goals and objectives of the vision fulfilled.

"When human beings meet together seeking the spirit with unity of purpose then they will also find their way to each other" (Rudolf Steiner).

Every team will inevitably experience times of trial, crisis, attacks and battles, where they will fail and incur losses. A good team will accept corporate responsibility for any failures and losses without seeking to blame-shift. These will not occur because the team intended them to, so they must be strong enough to embrace reality together. A good team will quickly seek how to manage the damage without letting emotions get out of control. It will be united in agreeing to let go and to move forward beyond their failures and losses. Any members or groups that try to distance themselves from the loss, liabilities and failures of the team are selfish and not real team players.

The strength in a team is seen not so much during victories as in failure. It is easy to be united in success, but altogether more difficult where there is failure and loss. A good servant will aim to unite their team during times of failures and loss. This is what true alignment looks like.

"We are only as strong as we are united, as weak as we are divided" (J. K. Rowling).

In a team there will be diverse views and opinions so a good team will respect one another and listen to one another's views and opinions.

"We cannot be separated in interest or divided in purpose. We stand together until the end" (Mattie Stepanek).

In any team, there will be members with different styles, methods and strategies and each must be accommodated and tested until the team unanimously arrives at the best way forward. A good servant will operate with respect towards the fellow servant and offer their views and opinions in humility. They will be open to accommodate the views and opinions of their fellow servants without being afraid to respectfully resist views and opinions that are not beneficial to the vision.

"Unity is strength…when there is teamwork and collaboration, wonderful things can be achieved" (Mattie Stepanek).

A good servant will speak the truth in love so that they do not discourage others while at the same time maintaining their integrity and embodying honesty. They will be mature enough to receive constructive criticism and gracious enough to also give it.

A good servant must align themselves to the unanimous decisions of the team unless they have a very valid reason to think that the other team members are derailing or deviating from the vision.

A good servant is a team player always eager to ensure that they are of one mind and one spirit with the other team members.

A good team player believes in and practices level 3 unity, which involves total alignment in spirit, mind and body.

The 7 Sevens

1. TO BUILD BOUNDARIES

To increase the speed of trust in a team, everyone needs to be aligned to the boundaries.

a) **What are boundaries and why are they important and necessary?**

"Boundaries are a part of self-care. They are healthy, normal, and necessary." (Doreen Virtue)

Personal boundaries are necessary and important to enable a servant to identify reasonable, safe and permissible ways for other people to behave towards them. They are also necessary to enable a servant to identify reasonable, safe and permissible ways of behaving towards other people. They help to guide you if someone crosses these boundaries.

b) **What are the different types and examples of personal boundaries?**

"Boundaries define us. They define what is me and what is not me. A boundary shows me where I end and someone else begins, leading me to a sense of ownership. Knowing what I am to own and take responsibility for gives me freedom." (Henry Cloud)

Here are some examples of personal boundaries:

Bodily contact: limiting how people can relate to your body, protecting you against inappropriate sexual contact and abuse.

Physical space: limiting how far people can access your space whether your home, office etc. This is designed to protect you against trespassing and intrusion.

Privacy and information: limiting how much of your personal information people can access which will protect you against people taking advantage of your generosity.

c) **How to maintain personal boundaries**

"You get what you tolerate." (Henry Cloud)

Here are some guidelines for keeping the boundaries secure:

- Constantly communicate and clarify your personal/boundaries to all concerned
- Promptly re-establish and rebuild any broken/or breached conditions
- Ensure that you are observing and respecting your co-servants and their personal boundaries

Establishing and building these boundaries will require you unapologetically, firmly and politely to communicate them to your co-servants. It will also require you to boldly but politely tell a fellow servant when they have crossed these personal borders.

2. TO CUT OUT CLIQUES

A) What are cliques and how are they formed?

"Don't give in to all the cliques and to popularity. It all means nothing. I know super popular guys, and guess what? They're just normal people too." (Leo Howard)

Cliques are toxic groups and cartels that possess a gang mentality. They are bullying and exclusive in nature, not readily allowing others to join. They often make others feel less important and valuable. They are held together by common interests and views, by people who have bonded together into a social network where there is usually a high degree of control being exercised. When cliques start to develop in a working environment, they can distract your focus from the main agenda, from your tasks and assignment. This can have a catastrophic effect on the unity and effectiveness of a team. Such cliques can quickly derail the social dynamics and cohesive unity of a group.

B) Why are cliques dangerous?

"I think life is more interesting when everybody's jumbled up together. When people separate out into cliques and things, it's okay, but it's a bit limiting. You can always learn things from other people." (Jarvis Cocker)

Cliques are dangerous because they obliterate people's individuality and pressurize people into negative actions and choices. This loss of individuality leads to an inability to make independent decisions. Furthermore, cliques by their very nature are closed groups, excluding and ostracizing others, thereby creating an atmosphere of mistrust. They distract servants from the goals of their servanthood and thereby seriously prejudice the leader and vision. They create illegitimate centres of power in which the loyalty of the servant is divided between the clique leader and the main leader. Finally, cliques are toxic because they also lead to favouritism, causing those who are not favoured to lose morale.

C) How to avoid cliques

A wise servant will steer away from unhealthy cliques in the workplace. They will refuse to pledge allegiance to any such group because their allegiance is to their leader and to the overarching vision. A wise servant will decline any invitation to join a clique politely but firmly, explaining that they are already so busy that they will not have time to meet the obligations of the clique, adding that they fear that the chances are high that they will end up disappointing them. Another tactic might be for a bold servant to confront a clique, depending on the position they hold in the team. A servant has an obligation to protect other weaker members of the team and so may explain to the clique how they prejudice the entire workforce.

3. TO CONTAIN CONFIDENTIALITY
a) Matters that fall within confidentiality

"Confidentiality is a virtue of the loyal, as loyalty is the virtue of faithfulness." (Edwin Louis Cole)

A servant will eventually be entrusted with confidential information by either the leader they are serving or by their co-servants. They must guard this entrustment if they are to remain trustworthy. They must avoid any co-servant who tends to break confidences lest they be found guilty of the same thing by association. As a servant, you must ask your leader and co-workers to outline what information is confidential and what is not. This will prevent you from denying relevant information to yourself or to others, or making you withhold information needed by others.

"Don't confuse 'strict confidentiality' with 'keeping employees in the dark.' Private is useful. Secretive is deceptive." (Stacy Feiner)

b) How to keep and maintain confidentiality

"If I maintain my silence about my secret, it is my prisoner...if I let it slip from my tongue, I am its prisoner." (Arthur Schopenhauer)

Here are a few practical guidelines for maintaining confidentiality:

- Discern what information and documents are classified as confidential so that you know exactly what you are guarding
- Determine how and where to store confidential information and documents
- Decide when you will need such information and who to release that information to

How to damage control after breaching confidentiality

"A secret spoken finds wings." (Robert Jordan)

Here are a few practical guidelines for dealing with breaches in confidentiality:

- Where a servant mistakenly breaches confidentiality, they must quickly and immediately report and own that breach to their superiors
- They must apologize sincerely and control the damage their breach may have caused as quickly as possible
- They must seek to understand exactly how the mistake in breaching occurred in order to avoid repeating it in the future

A Cautious Caveat

Notwithstanding the above, you must ensure that whatever you are being requested to keep confidential and secret does not have the potential to cause harm to the organization and to people or to lead to wrongdoing. Whatever you are keeping confidential should not lead to illegality or immorality. You should be free to refuse to be involved in the abuse of office, misuse of public funds, and so forth.

4. TO HONOUR HIERARCHY
a) What do we mean by hierarchy and rank?

"Without agreement on rank and a certain respect for authority there can be no great sensitivity to social rules, as anyone who has tried to teach simple house rules to a cat will agree!" (Frans de Waal)

Hierarchy refers to the chain of command in an organization. Such hierarchy exists for purposes of ensuring accountability. It denotes the levels of leadership, authority and responsibility in a team. Every group will have a pecking order where there are levels of authority (the *right* to do something) and power (the *might* to do something). In healthy organizations, hierarchy and rank are not about exploiting and oppressing people lower down the ladder but rather empowering and releasing them to exercise a form of servanthood that is joyful, free and productive – the best that it can be.

b) Why are hierarchy and rank important in the workplace?

"Honour is not the appendage of any social class. It is a way of life which may be freely chosen by any man or women, regardless of race, colour, or creed." (T. Braxton Woody)

Hierarchy establishes efficient communication paths and provides a reporting system in which every servant can benefit from reasonable supervision. A faithful servant must honour the hierarchy established by their leader, thereby demonstrating not only that they are a good follower, but also that they will likely one day make a good leader. A servant's ability to honour authority and hierarchy also demonstrates their humility and teachability. Their ability to honour hierarchy demonstrates that their respect for their leader's authority is genuine. Their respect for their leader is also clearly signposted by their readiness to honour those to whom the leader has delegated authority. It is dishonest for a servant to say that they honour and respect the authority of the leader while not being prepared to respect those whom the leader has given a measure of authority within the organization.

c) How to observe hierarchy and ranks

A respectful servant will seek to understand the hierarchy and the ranks within the organization so that they do not step out of line and cause destruction. They will seek to understand the roles and responsibilities and mandates of those in the hierarchy. They will relate in a respectful way to their superiors through their speech, posture and action. They will seek to understand the temperaments of those in authority.

A Cautious Caveat

While the above is true, you must ensure that the rank and hierarchy that you are required to honour is legitimate and not self-imposed. It must not be oppressive or hinder you from fulfilling your purpose. There are cases where faithful servants will encounter a supervisor who lords it over them, thereby hampering and hindering their growth. You must be free to expose and reject such illegitimate and oppressive uses of authority and power.

5. TO EXERCISE EMOTIONAL INTELLIGENCE
a) What is emotional intelligence?

"There are certain emotions that will kill your drive, such as frustration and confusion. You can change these to a positive

force. Frustration means you are on the verge of a breakthrough. Confusion can mean you are about to learn something. Expect the breakthrough and expect to learn." (Kathleen Spike)

Emotional intelligence (sometimes referred to as EQ) is the individual's ability to recognize and regulate their own emotions, especially in relationship to others in the organization. It is the ability to discern and distinguish between different feelings and label them appropriately. The main components of emotional intelligence are self-awareness, self-regulation, self-management, self-motivation, social skills and empathy.

Self-awareness is the ability to recognize an emotion when you experience it. This is the key to emotional intelligence. Self-regulation and self-management refer to the ability to control one's emotions and impulses to avoid acting irrationally and making careless decisions.

Self-motivation is your capacity to stir yourself to action by harnessing your negative emotions and turning them into a positive force.

Social skills refer to your ability to interact, relate to, and communicate with others using right social conventions, with rapport and etiquette, relying on proper verbal and body languages being aware of your emotions, and theirs.

Empathy is the ability to be sensitive, to share the feelings of another, to place oneself in another's position. If sympathy denotes your ability to feel *for* someone else (with compassion and pity), empathy denotes your ability to feel *with* them.

When dealing with your fellow servants, you must develop and exercise these traits of healthy EQ. These will help you to excel in conflict management and dispute resolution.

b) **Why is emotional intelligence necessary when dealing with co-workers?**

"It isn't stress that makes us fall–it's how we respond to stressful events." (Wayde Goodall)

Dealing with people without adequate EQ will often result in fighting unnecessary battles. A servant with low EQ is likely to sabotage their own efforts by misreading situations, distorting facts and adopting negative self-limitations. Lack of EQ will cause an otherwise capable servant to mishandle people and situations.

c) How to deal with or respond to fellow workers with low emotional intelligence

"Emotional intelligence is the ability to sense, understand, and effectively apply the power and acumen of emotions as a source of human energy, information, connection, and influence." (Robert K. Cooper)

A wise servant will ensure that they do not descend to a low level of EQ. Instead, they will be intentional about cultivating and operating with high levels of EQ, acting as an example to their fellow servants by avoiding unnecessary conflict. They may choose to help a fellow servant to upgrade their EQ by sharing the knowledge they have acquired about managing their emotions, and the benefits this has given. They may elect to avoid fellow servants with low EQ so as not to be associated with sources of dissension.

6. TO SEE THE GOLD NOT THE GARBAGE
a) **What is the gold?**

"Everything has beauty, but not everyone sees it." (Confucius)

One does not need a special gift to see the garbage in others. However, one needs a special gift to see the gold. Gold in this context symbolizes that which is precious and valuable in other people, such as their unique gifts, talents, anointings, skill sets, good qualities, admirable values, and so on.

b) What is the garbage?

Garbage in this context symbolizes that which is vile, negative, despicable, base, loathsome and weak. Those who focus on the garbage focus on people's negative proclivities and visible shortcomings. A mature servant must learn to differentiate between difficult people and different people and embrace their diversity. The ability to feed the gold in another person and the ability to starve the garbage in them is what will make your servanthood stand above that of others.

c) How to bring out the gold so that it outshines the garbage

A good servant will highlight to his fellow servant their strengths and gifts, thereby encouraging them to focus on their positive traits and to use them. They will assign roles and responsibilities to that servant that are in alignment with their strengths and gifts. They will be aware that they are building human souls not soulless stones. In their servanthood, they will know that people are more important than projects. They will give moral and social support to fellow servants and share criticism wisely, as well as receive it graciously. They will learn to identify and elicit the gold in people while managing and dealing with the garbage. They will learn to empower and positively influence others so that they are better off than they were when they first met them.

"No matter where we come from, there is one language we can all speak and understand from birth, the language of the heart, love." *(Imania Margria)*

Promoting the gold in others is one of the strongest and most powerful ways of uniting people because it involves the good servant speaking the language of love. Love is forbearing and patient with the garbage, not keeping records of wrongs. It entails acts of kindness, applying gentleness in all your actions and sensitivity.

Love means not being self-seeking or having inflated egos but rather being selfless and having other people's interests at heart. Tough love may sometimes be necessary because an open rebuke is better than a hidden flattering tongue. But the key here will be speaking the truth in love.

Love requires creating trust and rebuilding trust where it has been broken by extending grace and being ready to overlook mistakes and offences (garbage).

Love requires accommodating the weakness of others, avoiding a judgemental spirit, edifying and building up as opposed to being critical and oppressive.

Love entails not using your position of influence to undermine others or lording it over others. The most important yardstick of your success will be how you treat people –your family, friends and co-workers, and even strangers you meet along the way.

Love entails celebrating the success of others, not being jealous of those victories, or seeking to take the credit for them. Love focuses on the gold. It does not fixate on the garbage.

7. TO SAFEGUARD YOUR INNER SANCTUARY
A) What is your sanctuary?

Your sanctuary is your heart, the seat of your emotions. It is a sacred place where you keep your deepest, most intimate thoughts and feelings.

B) Why should you guard your sanctuary?

During your servanthood, in view of the various dynamics you will encounter in the place of your servanthood and among your co-servants, you must learn to guard your sanctuary, the sacred centre within. You must protect your heart from being excessively hurt. You guard it by regularly retreating when threats to your security and serenity arise.

A good servant must guard against being defiled by any toxic or negative behaviour from any of their co-servants. They must guard against being distracted and derailed from their mission. They will keep a song in their sanctuary – a song they will sing to themselves to drown out all the noise from outside.

C) What are the dangers of an unguarded sanctuary?

When a servant fails to guard their sanctuary, they will experience the pain of being mishandled and mistreated by fellow workers. Such hurts can cripple and paralyze them in their servanthood and render them unproductive. Extreme woundedness may lead a servant to become bitter, angry and negative, to start seeking revenge against a fellow servant, this is always counter-productive for themselves and their team.

Thought Provoking Questions for Discussion

1. What challenges have you had in building boundaries and how do you think you can learn to build effective boundaries?

2. What challenges have you had in cutting out cliques and how do you think you can learn how to maintain a clique-free team?

3. What challenges have you had in ensuring confidentiality and how do you think you can learn to enhance confidentiality?

4. What challenges have you had in upholding honour and hierarchy and how do you think you can learn to build honour?

5. What challenges have you had in exercising emotional intelligence and how do you think you can learn to build more effective emotional intelligence in yourself and your team?

6. What challenges have you had in identifying the gold and not the garbage in others and how do you think you can learn to improve in this vital, team-enriching virtue?

7. What challenges have you had in safeguarding your sanctuary and how do you think you can learn to do this more effectively?

SEVEN WAYS OF RELATING WITH YOUR LEADER

"It is the men behind who make the man ahead." (Merle Crowell)

In order to be effective and successful in serving the leader and the vision, you must be able to relate to them appropriately and strategically. The relationship between you and your leader may often be challenging and complex; it is your correct positioning and alignment in that relationship that will make all the difference. To do this, you must be able to discern the varied dispositions of your leader in order to know how to relate and respond to them appropriately in and out of season. Your leader may manifest different traits depending on their calling and the context.

The creatures that surround the throne in revelation chapter 4 give us symbols for these traits: the eagle (symbolizing prophetic and visionary leadership), the lion (symbolizing courageous leadership), the ox (symbolizing strong, burden-bearing leadership), and the man (symbolizing humane and compassionate leadership). Your task is to discern which of these roles your leader is embracing, which of these temperaments they are displaying, during the different seasons of their leadership journey. Your role in relation to their calling will depend upon which of these kinds of leaders they are at this moment. What they are determines what you need to become for them.

In this regard, there are seven positions you can take up in relation to your leader. These positions are not dependent upon what you want or need. They are entirely reliant upon what your leader wants and needs. If the season is one of stabilising the organisation, healing hurts and recovering from loss, then the leader will need to be more pastoral and compassionate, displaying the face of the man and the backbone of the ox. Your role will be to support them in that, doing everything you can to help the team and the people served by the leader and their vision to recover. If, however, the leader is in ground-taking and pioneering mode, then you will need to embrace a position and posture that serves that season and strategy. In this mode, the leader may be manifesting the face of an eagle and the roar of the lion. Where you stand and serve will be defined and determined by that, not by what you want to be doing during this strategic season.

In what follows, we are going to be looking at the seven positions you as a servant may take up in relation to your leader, depending on their situation and their temperament. You must demonstrate that you can be flexible in adapting to their character and context. A great servant never tries to mould the leader into what they need them to be. The great servant morphs into what their leader needs them to be.

The 7 Sevens

1. BEHIND

There are some seasons in which a good servant needs to be positioned **behind** their leader both physically (as someone following them) and spiritually (as someone submitted to their lead). From this position, the servant can cover their leader's back and cheer them on as they lead the people forward. From this position, you can both affirm and defend your leader. When you get behind your leader, you are acknowledging that the leader takes the lead and a servant follows. You are also showing that you back up and are behind your leader's decisions whenever there is internal or external opposition. A good time to be behind your leader is whenever they are enduring a crisis of confidence. This may follow battles or failures that have left them emotionally and mentally paralyzed, leading to a temporary loss of focus. In these times when a leader can lose momentum and energy, a faithful servant must be fully behind them if the leader is to be propelled forward again.

2. BESIDE

A good servant at other times should be positioned **beside** their leader. This conveys that the servant's heart is on and at the leader's side. It also communicates the fact that the leader regards the servant as so trustworthy that they can be at their right or left hand. From the servant's point of view, being beside the leader is an affirmation of their support. From the leader's point of view, the servant being permitted to walk beside them is an affirmation of their confidence in that person.

Albert Camus wrote, *"Don't walk behind me; I may not lead. Don't walk in front of me; I may not follow. Just walk beside me and be my friend."*

Obviously, a servant must maintain appropriate boundaries in this position so that they do not become overfamiliar with the leader, implying equality rather than hierarchy. The servant must always remember that friendship will need in any case to take a back seat when this season comes to an end. Such a season usually coincides with the leader undergoing a personal or emotional challenge in which they become vulnerable and exposed. In those times, they may need to lean on you more, treating you more as a peer and a friend than a servant. This close, the leader can use you as a sounding board for ideas as well as a source of comfort, strength, reassurance and help. Do not let the leader's vulnerability become an invitation for overfamiliarity. Do not let their treatment of you as a peer become the fertile soil for pride to grow in your life.

3. AHEAD

A good servant at other times will need to be positioned **ahead** or in front of their leader in order to go ahead and spy out, assess and clear away any obstacles. In this situation, the good servant is exercising a reconnaissance ministry. They are not in any sense going ahead to lead their leader. They are in that position as a scout, risking everything self-sacrificially to prevent the leader from being bounced or ambushed. This, then, is a thoroughly humble position. You are not ahead of the leader to boost your ego or your status. You are there to give a big shout-out to your leader, not to take the glory. Sometimes, going ahead of your leader can be for the purpose of announcing and heralding the arrival of the leader.

In this respect, you are like another forerunner and servant John the Baptist, saying, "I must decrease; he must increase!" You are preparing the way for your leader, making sure that everyone is ready to receive them. You prepare the ground of people's hearts too. The able servant creates an atmosphere of welcome. This kind of position is mainly taken up when the leader is in pioneering mode, taking new ground, advancing new ideas. The servant absorbs some of the blows associated with this kind of major transition. Why? So that the leader does not have to suffer these blows themselves.

4. ABOVE

There will also be times when a good servant will be positioned **above** their leader for purposes of 'covering,' which means shielding their honour and integrity. It will never be for lording it over the leader. This kind of position is necessary where, for example, a servant is intervening, interceding or intercepting matters on behalf of their leader. You position yourself above in order to protect them from being exposed to situations where there might be ugly verbal exchanges or unbecoming behaviour. Being positioned above them during such times means that the servant will protect the leader by taking the fiery darts that are thrown at them. This is part and parcel of your servanthood. You cannot shy away from it. Being positioned above your leader also means taking on the role of lookout or observer, establishing a higher vantage point from which the servant becomes more aware of what is going on, both positively and negatively. This watchman role gives the servant the ability to become cognizant of the issues that the leader is either facing or going to have to face. You do this in order to take necessary action.

5. AROUND

A good servant should at times be positioned **around** their leader for protection and cover.

Being positioned around means that the servant is establishing themselves as a human shield. If you think about it, positioning yourself above the leader will often lead you to position yourself around them. Once you see what is coming against them, you can set up a hedge of protection around them. It also means that you help to support and enhance what they need at different times and seasons. Being around your leader enables you to add to the right-brain qualities of analytical and methodical thinking, and to the left-brain qualities of creativity and innovation. As a servant, you need to be well rounded if you are to be around the leader. As Howard Schultz, CEO of Starbucks, has said:

"When you're surrounded by people who share a passionate commitment around a common purpose, anything is possible."

Being around your leader is symptomatic of your accessibility. Your proximity sends a signal about your availability. Your leader should be able to see and feel your positive presence around them, symbolically and physically.

6. APART

A good servant needs to discern the times when they should be positioned away or **apart** from their leader to give them space and privacy to reflect, ponder and rest. Being apart prevents you from suffocating and stifling them. You will need to learn to discern when your leader needs time with their family, friends, other servants and other people generally. When you mess up and grieve your leader, it is important that you step aside and lie low for a while to give your leader time to cool off and heal before you reconnect. However, a servant must be careful not to distance themselves too far or for too long. When that happens, you may fail to discern the time to reconnect. That said, you should make sure that you do not commit any offence that could lead to a permanent disconnection.

7. WITHIN

It is important for a good servant to get **within** their leader's head, seeing the world from their perspective, understanding what makes them tick, why they think the way they do. This involves empathy. What is on their mind needs to be on yours too.

Getting inside your leader's head enables you to be proactive because you more and more learn the way they think. It is a joy for a leader when a servant-hearted follower takes the necessary action before they even instruct them. Knowing how a leader thinks, how they feel, what excites them, what grieves them, what energises them and what depletes them, what causes them to be happy and what makes them downcast, is one of the ways that a servant can transition from good to great. The more you get inside your leader's thinking, the more likely you are to enter the inner core of people who advises them.

"The quality of your life is determined by the quality of your servanthood" (Will Smith).

Out of these seven ways of relating to your leader, which ones have you found most challenging in your experience?

In your opinion, are all these seven ways necessary or are there some that you can do away with and still serve your leader effectively?

Is there any one or more ways out of these seven that have been counterproductive in your experience?

Which of these seven ways have you now realized you have not been relating to your leader with?

What other ways beyond these seven do you believe are beneficial and if so, why?

Have you ever served a leader who objected to you relating to them in any one of these ways, if so, what were the objections?

Is it possible that you have not been relating to your leader in any one of these ways and in your opinion do you think not doing so has resulted in a less effective servanthood?

Chapter 6

THE PROCESS OF SERVANTHOOD

Embracing Your Development Into a Premium Servant

"Success is not measured by what you accomplish, but by the opposition you have encountered, and the courage with which you have maintained the struggle against overwhelming odds." ~ Orison Swett Marden

Chapter Outline

7 Test and Temptations

1. Familiarity
2. Offence
3. Greed
4. Undermining the Authority of a Principal
5. Serving With Fatigue
6. Confidentiality Breaches
7. Exceeding Mandate

7 Seasons of a Servant

1. Persecution
2. Rejection
3. Exploitation
4. Purging and Threshing
5. Attacks and Battles
6. Rest to Replenish
7. Promotion (Harvest)

7 Right Positioning At Your Place

1. Your Mind-set
2. Your Eyes
3. Your Ears
4. Your Mouth
5. Your Heart
6. Your Hands
7. Your Feet

INTRODUCTION

Becoming a seasoned servant is a process which you must embrace. Receiving the call to serve is one thing, but your character, gifting and skills will need to be formed and harnessed over time. Provided you are committed, open and willing to become more and more effective in your servanthood, then your formation will propel you to levels of effectiveness beyond your dreams.

The process is, of course, painful and sometimes you may feel you cannot take anymore. You may be tempted to quit but you must keep in mind that the process is necessary and without it your servanthood will at best be mediocre.

In this chapter, we will start by examining the seven tests you will need to pass, such as over-familiarity, offence, greed, undermining the authority of your leader, servanthood fatigue, breaches of confidentiality and exceeding your mandate.

We will then examine seven seasons you will need to undergo, such as seasons of persecution, rejection, exploitation, purging, pruning and threshing, warfare, rest and promotion. You will learn how to discern the nature of every season, to position yourself correctly with the right attitudes in that season, to identify and relate to the various people you will encounter in that season, to escape the traps and snares in that season, to apply the important lessons from that season, and to transition from that season, propelling yourself to the next season.

Finally, we will examine seven radical surgeries you will need to undergo in seven key areas in order to refine you for your service. These are your mind (symbolizing your mind-set and thoughts), your eyes (symbolizing your vision), your ears (symbolizing your ability to hear), your nose (symbolizing your discernment), your mouth (symbolizing your words and speech), your heart (symbolizing your emotions), your hands (symbolizing your work), and your feet (symbolizing your walk and lifestyle).

The key to effective service lies in your ability to respond correctly to these tests, seasons and surgeries and to allow them to mould and sculpture you into a premium servant. Failure to respond to and handle these challenges correctly may mean that you consign yourself to ineffective and mediocre service, or that you end up aborting your servanthood altogether. Neither of these outcomes is what you need or want.

So, then, let us begin with the seven tests that a servant commonly experiences as they undergo the process of being formed into a premium servant.

THE 7 TESTS A SERVANT WILL NEED TO PASS IN THE PROCESS OF THEIR FORMATION

"A successful man is one who can lay a firm foundation with the bricks others have thrown at him" (David Brinkley).

During the journey of your servanthood, you will encounter a myriad of circumstances, situations, pressures and stresses where your character, core values, motives and loyalties will be tested to the maximum. Your ability to withstand the fiery furnace, overcome the temptations and escape the traps in your way will usher you into higher levels of effectiveness in your servanthood.

The tests we are about to look at will arise primarily out of the relationship between you and the leader you are serving. The key here is to guard very carefully how you respond and handle yourself during these tests.

Some wrong reactions you may be tempted to adopt are as follows:

a) Using silence and sulking as a weapon to frustrate your leader.

b) Emotionally blackmailing your leader to see your leader fail.

c) Practicing a passive-aggressive mode whereby you adopt a go-slow policy and you remove yourself mentally and emotionally, even if you are there physically.

d) Practicing an active-aggressive mode whereby you resort to dramatic confrontations bordering on serious insubordination and disrespect.

These are just some of the wrong reactions. No matter how tough the times get and how challenging the tests become, you must always guard against bad mouthing your leader.

Also, beware of inappropriate confrontation. You must confront issues honestly by checking your own motives first, addressing your dissatisfaction privately and maturely with your leader.

In *The Book of Numbers* chapter 16, we find one of Moses's servants called Korah dishonouring Moses by confronting him publicly. Korah's conduct is in stark contrast to David who prostrated himself before King Saul privately, disarming himself as a sign of humility. Watch your body language and never attack your leader.

The 7 Sevens

1. FAMILIARITY

"The Law of Familiarity: People feel comfortable with who and what they know." (Michelle Tillis Lederman)

What is Familiarity?

Familiarity in this context means a relaxed friendliness or intimacy. Over-familiarity means being unduly forward or brash, offensively presumptuous, excessively friendly or intimate, taking undue liberties. It can be manifested in your tone and language, in your use of physical contact, or in the kind of information you divulge to your leader.

"Familiarity breeds contempt" (Mark Twain).

Serving a leader for a long time can make you so aware of their faults that you become disrespectful. The more you know someone, the more you see their weaknesses. Sometimes a leader's warmth can lead a servant to mistakenly assume that they are being offered an invitation to ease the boundaries of propriety and to become forward. At other times, over-familiarity can come out of a time when a leader drops their guard in a moment of vulnerability, disclosing deep personal issues to their servant. The servant then foolishly sees this as a license to become over-familiar and overly personal.

"Familiarity makes the lion more dangerous" (Jocelyn Murray).

How to Avoid Becoming Over-Familiar

A wise servant will constantly remind themselves who or what their leader is, and they will also remind themselves of their own place under that leader. They will maintain boundaries and understand that being able to see their leader's faults is an opportunity to know them better in order to serve them better, not a reason to erode respect. Remember, you can never benefit from an authority that you do not respect.

2. OFFENCE

"Love the offender yet detest the offence." (Alexander Pope)

What is offence?

Offence refers to feelings of resentment caused by a perceived insult. It is inevitable that over the course of your servanthood, situations will arise where a leader may upset their servant knowingly or unknowingly. An offended servant has a choice how to respond to that offence, and ultimately it is their response that will determine the effect that this perceived offence will have on them.

The wrong response is to become angry, bitter and resentful, and to start serving with a bad attitude, which releases toxicity into the atmosphere around you. Your servanthood then becomes substandard. You disconnect from the leader and the vision emotionally. You end up disengaging physically, removing yourself from your place of assignment, aborting God's purposes. The right response is to recognize that every offence is a snare and to seek the grace to overlook that offence, forgive the offender and resume your positive servanthood. If the need and time to discuss it with the leader arises for purposes of healing, then seize the moment but do so respectfully and graciously.

How to Avoid the Snare of Offence

"An honest man speaks the truth, though it may give offence; a vain man, in order that it may." (William Hazlitt)

An emotionally mature servant will keep in mind that their leader is human and not perfect. They will remember and focus on the bigger picture, namely the vision they are serving. They will not allow smaller issues, like personal feelings of resentment, to become like little foxes that ruin the vineyard. They remember that offences will inevitably happen but that overlooking them is a sign of maturity.

3. GREED

"Greed is a bottomless pit which exhausts the person in an endless effort to satisfy the need without ever reaching satisfaction." (Erich Fromm)

Greed is another test.

What is Greed?

Greed is the intense and selfish desire for something, especially wealth, power, position and status. Greed is an appetite that causes you to desire something for which you are not yet ready.

A Biblical example is Lot. Lot did not want to continue serving Abraham because he wanted to go on his own before he was ready to do so, which caused him to abort his purpose and destiny. In the marketplace today, a servant may think they are ready to start their own business. They may disconnect from serving in another person's business and then end up failing miserably. Sometimes, young and immature professionals seek to go off on their own without having developed enough character or competence to do so. They end up becoming embezzlers and defrauders of their clients and customers. A servant gripped by greed cannot be trusted to be a good steward of their leader's resources. Greed leads to theft and deception which will ultimately undermine and prejudice the vision they are serving. When a servant is greedy for power, position and status, they will succumb to selfish ambitions, interests and agendas instead of promoting and advancing the interests of the leader and vision. This will lead to a conflict between the interests of their leader and their own.

How to Avoid the Snare of Greed

A servant must constantly remind themselves that their calling is to serve the vision of another until such time as God opens the door for them to step out on their own. Materialism and greed for mammon lead to destruction.

"Greed is the inventor of injustice as well as the current enforcer" *(Julian Casablancas).*

4. UNDERMINING THE AUTHORITY OF A PRINCIPAL

This is where the servant erodes their leader's authority in the eyes of others through

- Negative criticism of instructions and decisions
- Murmuring and complaining against the leader
- Questioning the leader's instructions and decisions
- Passing judgment on the leader's actions

What Causes this Behaviour?

This kind of behaviour derives from feelings of superiority in which a servant believes they know more than their leader and that they can lead better than the leader is doing. This then causes the servant to possess a misguided sense of entitlement, a false sense of self-importance in which they think their leader should consult them in decision making, a desire to "perfect" the leader through manipulation and control, and a tendency to incite others into doubting the leader's abilities. Someone who has these symptoms will also mislead others into defying the leader's instructions, they will erode people's confidence in the leader's authority, dilute the leader's influence, delay the progress of the vision, provoke and incite others to rebellion against the leader, fail the test and end up in destruction.

How to avoid the temptation to undermine the leader's authority

A reverent servant must guard their heart and mouth against any sentiments and utterances that seek to undermine their leader in any way. They must purpose to remain loyal. They must channel all their concerns through the proper, laid-down procedures and do so in a mature and sincere manner.

5. SERVING WITH FATIGUE

"Anxiety happens when you think you have to figure out everything all at once. Breathe. You're strong. You got this. Take it day by day." (Karen Salmansohn)

What is Servanthood Fatigue?

At the end of the day, even the best of servants is still human, so it is natural for them to reach a point of weariness and exhaustion, to lose the joy of serving and to begin to feel unfulfilled and demotivated. This can happen when the tasks and assignments become mundane, routine and boring, when the servant feels unappreciated and taken for granted, when the rewards of servanthood appear remote and elusive, when the servant begins to feel that they have given out much more than they have received, when they have become worn out on the battlefield after an intense season of attacks and warfare.

Some of the symptoms of fatigue are the following:

- A loss of focus
- An abandonment of one's assignment
- A premature disconnection from one's leader
- A mental and emotional breakdown
- A resentment and bitterness which open doors to a myriad of bad choices and errors of judgment with devastating consequences.

How to Avoid Servanthood Fatigue

As a sensitive servant, you should aim to do the following:

- Live a balanced life, setting aside time to rest and recuperate
- Learn to encourage yourself by keeping a song in your heart
- Avoid expecting accolades and remind yourself that your labour of love can never be in vain
- Manage or erase any misplaced expectations to avoid unnecessary disappointment
- Reach out to your encouragers for much-needed moral support

6. CONFIDENTIALITY BREACHES

"Confidentiality is a virtue of the loyal, as loyalty is the virtue of faithfulness." (Edwin Louis Cole)

What are Breaches of Confidentiality?

This happens when information given in confidence to a servant is disclosed by them to other people without the leader's consent. This disclosure can be done intentionally and maliciously, or unintentionally and accidentally. This also happens when a servant fails to respect their leader's privacy, resulting in a violation of the trust and confidence the leader had placed in that servant.

Trust and confidentiality may either be verbally accepted by a servant or written in the form of a non-disclosure agreement signed by the servant. Oftentimes, confidentiality is implicit and obvious just by virtue of the sensitive nature of the information. In those cases, a servant should know that it is wrong to disclose it.

"Confidentiality is an ancient and well-warranted social value" (Kay Redfield Jamison).

When this social value is neglected, confidentialities can be breached in the following situations:

- Where a servant is careless with what they say
- Where a servant spends time with the wrong company and is then enticed and deceived into disclosing information
- Where a servant decides to prove their relevance and their closeness to a leader by showing off and in the process discloses information that makes them look more important
- Where a servant succumbs to greed and ambition and is seduced into compromising their leader
- Where a servant is threatened and seeks to protect themselves and their interests by throwing their leader under the bus, forgetting that one of their fundamental responsibilities is to shield the leader

The only exception to this is when a leader has committed criminal acts. In these situations, the servant should seek advice.

How to Avoid Breaches in Confidentiality and Trust

A faithful servant must always guard their mouth and be slow to speak. They must be careful in how they store and safeguard their leader's documents and information. They must be careful about who they associate with and discern insincere and impure motives in others. They must remain secure in who they are so that they have no need to show off and boast to prove their relevance and value. They must avoid greed and be ready to suffer for their leader, protecting them at all costs. They must be very vigilant and cautious, knowing that breaches of confidentiality will increase their leader's vulnerability, which a faithful servant is always supposed to cover.

"In intelligence work, there are limits to the amount of information one can share. Confidentiality is essential." (Gijs de Vries)

7. EXCEEDING YOUR MANDATE

"We must learn to accept the calling God has given us. Develop a clear understanding of what God has called you to do, stay in your lane and find value in your part in God's ultimate plan." (T. D. Jakes)

What Does Exceeding Your Mandate Mean?

A servant should be one who operates according to the instructions of another. Everything they say and do should be on behalf of another because they are serving someone else's vision. Sometimes an overzealous servant may become overconfident and overstep their scope of duty and their mandate. This can prejudice the interests of their leader. A servant can overstep his mandate when.

- They begin to imagine they are at the same level as their leader, that they are a "vision co-bearer", a full partner.
- They do not understand their scope.
- They want to impress others.
- They become impatient with their leader's perceived indecisions and procrastinations.
- They begin knowingly or unknowingly to hijack the leader's vision

How to Avoid Exceeding Your Mandate

A good servant takes steps to avoid this pitfall by ensuring that they clearly understand their place, the scope of their mandate and their terms of reference. A good servant should regularly review and remind themselves of these.

The servant will empower themselves to avoid exceeding their mandate in the following ways:

- By remembering to ask whenever they are not sure about the limits of their mandate, instead of being presumptuous and assuming they know.
- By remembering that the leader is the vision bearer and that they (the servant) are the supporter of the vision.
- By remembering that all fundamental decisions must be made by the vision bearer.
- By remembering that their role and duty is to serve as a representative and mouthpiece for their leader, speaking and doing what they are instructed to speak and do, not their own words and actions.

Thought Provoking Questions for Discussion

1. Have there been instances when you have found yourself being over-familiar with your leader? What were the consequences and how did you redeem yourself?

2. Have there been instances when you have found yourself offending your leader? What were the consequences and how did you redeem yourself?

3. Have there been instances when you have found yourself trapped with greed in your servanthood? What were the consequences and how did you redeem yourself?

4. Have there been instances when you have found yourself undermining the authority of your leader? What were the consequences and how did you redeem yourself?

5. Have there been instances when you have found yourself fatigued in your servanthood? What were the consequences and how did you redeem yourself?

6. Have there been instances when you have found yourself breaching confidentiality in your servanthood? What were the consequences and how did you redeem yourself?

7. Have there been instances when you have found yourself exceeding the mandate expected of you in your servanthood and what were the consequences? How did you redeem yourself?

THE 7 SEASONS IN SERVANTHOOD

As a faithful servant, you must discern the different seasons of your servanthood by understanding the nature of each season you may find yourself in and discovering its purpose. You need to know how you should position yourself during that season by adopting the correct and appropriate attitudes and by identifying the different kinds of people you will encounter, knowing in the process how to relate to each one. You must also discern and learn the lessons you are supposed to learn from each season. You must know when the time has come to transition from one season to another. You must also be alert to the traps in each season, knowing how to escape them. As a wise servant, you will have to understand some fundamentals about the seasons of servanthood, namely:

1. That everything has seasons and so does your servanthood
2. That seasons come in cycles and every season must come to an end, so you must learn to see the whole cycle to avoid being crushed by one season
3. That each season is unique
4. That one season can balance another, supplying favour in place of famine
5. That you cannot prevent or manipulate the seasons
6. That your role is to change and adjust yourself to fit the seasons
7. That you must embrace each season and allow it to sculpt, mould and grow you into a better servant.
8. That you must master and command each season to work in your favour
9. That you must allow yourself to evolve and grow in each season
10. That you must ensure you do the right thing in the right season
11. That you do not miss the opportunities of any season and that if you do, you must learn how to redeem the missed season.

The 7 Sevens

1. THE SEASON OF PERSECUTION

"It is unjust, but only Christlike, to suffer persecution for doing what is right." (Joyce Rachelle)

The Nature of the Season

Persecution is a season when, as a servant, you suffer for doing what is right. This can involve systemic victimization or sporadic mistreatment. In this season, you may experience injustices, oppression, discrimination, harassment, alienation, and attempts to disqualify your servanthood. The persecution may be ignited by your faith, race, values, political views, or any other real or imaginary reason.

What is the purpose of this season?

It is to cleanse you of self-elevation and self-righteousness, especially when you feel you are performing well, and you have allowed pride to infiltrate your heart.

"The time of persecution and opposition is a time of cleansing" (Sunday Adelaja).

Such seasons test your capacity to handle hardships and injustices, to stand firm without compromising the truth in trouble and trials, and to hold fast to the vision

How to be positioned in this season

In order to successfully navigate this season, you must try to do the following:

1. Develop patience
2. Yield graciously to show that you are superior to your persecutor

3. Allow God to judge, defend and vindicate you
4. Continue to submit and remain faithful
5. Remain focused and steadfast in your servanthood
6. Respond in kindness, courtesy and tolerance
7. Rejoice in a quiet and humble way

How to Relate Appropriately to the Different People You'll Encounter in this Season

The first character you encounter in this season is obviously your persecutor. This person is often someone intimidated by your success and who seeks to persecute you for the beliefs and values that have enabled you to be effective. Your persecutor will hate and despise these beliefs and values. They may even want you to forsake them and maybe embrace their own. The most appropriate way to relate to your persecutor is to stand firm on your beliefs and values without any aggression. You should respond without engaging in wrongdoing. If they throw you in the lion's den, so be it.

The second character you encounter is the person being persecuted with you and who is not strong enough to withstand the season. They end up compromising and turning into your persecutor as well. You relate to them as you would relate to the persecutor.

The third is also the one being persecuted with you, but in their case, they stand firm just like you do, refusing to compromise. You relate to them as your allies, resolving to be supportive towards them in your common sufferings.

The fourth is also the one who is being persecuted with you and who is not strong enough to resist. However, this person does not betray you and they do not turn into your persecutor. You relate to them with compassion, refusing to be judgemental towards them because your strength is not their strength.

What Snares and Traps are You Likely to Encounter in this Season?

There are four common pitfalls you need to avoid during a season of persecution:

1. The temptation to compromise and forsake your beliefs and values
2. The temptation to fight your persecutor and respond with aggression and end up destroyed
3. The temptation to engage in wrongdoing in defending and protecting yourself
4. The temptation to mock and judge those who compromise out of weakness. This will make you self-righteous and cruel.

What Lessons Should You Take Away From This Season?

Always remember that persecution happens to the servant who is doing the right thing. In Mark 4:16-18, Jesus teaches that some people are like seeds sown on rocky ground. They hear the word and at once receive it with joy. But they themselves have no root, and they remain for only a season. When trouble or persecution comes because of the word, they quickly fall away. Remember that persecution proves the authenticity of your faith and your work. It develops maturity in you and moulds your character.

My brethren, count it all joy when you fall into various trials, knowing that the testing of your faith produces patience. But let patience have its perfect work, that you may be [perfect and complete, lacking nothing]. (James 1:2-4)

Joseph underwent trials in the form of jealousy from his brothers. This resulted in slavery and false accusations by Potiphar's wife (Genesis 37 and 39). However, these trials prepared him for becoming the leader of Egypt, where he excelled and exemplified godly character.

Resolve to learn and apply every lesson you are supposed to learn during the season of persecution. These lessons are redemptive gifts.

How to Time Your Transition from this Season

Every season has an end. There is therefore a danger of remaining in one season too long. This may destroy you or drive you into a destructive comfort zone where you accept your circumstances and give up. You will know that this season is coming to an end

- When your persecutor becomes weary of persecuting you as they see your determination in holding your ground
- When you see your persecutor softening towards you as they begin to accept and embrace your beliefs and values
- When you have stood firm without compromising and you have grown in maturity and character and you have learnt the lessons of that season.

2. THE SEASON OF REJECTION

"A rejection is nothing more than a necessary step in the pursuit of success." (Bo Bennett)

The Nature of this Season

Rejection denotes the act of refusing to accept or believe in someone. It is deliberately treating someone in a way that shows you care nothing for them and regard them as worthless. The results of rejection are isolation, depression, discouragement, despair and feeling abandoned. When a servant is rejected by their leader, this may either be because they have punished you for some wrongdoing or because the leader's own insecurity has caused them to make a false accusation against you.

What is the Purpose of this Season?

Rejection is an opportunity not just a difficulty – an opportunity to train yourself as a servant to be secure in who you are, and to accept and love yourself. It is also an opportunity to purge yourself of any clinginess, dependency and obsessiveness in relation to your leader. It offers, in other words, a time to reflect and to grow in self-awareness.

How Should You be Positioned in this Season

There are four essential attitudes that you need to use like garments to clothe your mind during a season of rejection. You must

- Remain faithful without hitting out at your leader, or disconnecting from or abandoning your servanthood
- Stay submitted and focused on your servanthood
- Be alert and cautious, knowing when to be low and keep your distance from your leader for a while
- Remember that a season is exactly that - a season - and it will pass

How to relate appropriately to the different characters in this season

1) With your Leader

The primary person you will encounter in this season is your leader, or the leadership you have been serving. Your response to their rejection is to maintain a stance of loyalty and positivity, remaining faithful to those in authority and refusing to be negative about them. The worst thing you can do is to fight rejection with rejection. Do not be proud and resentful. It will be your humility and kindness that will cause them to want you back.

2) Your Co-Workers

The secondary group will be fellow workers and your response to them is to continue collaborating and co-labouring with them. Exhibit a mature attitude by resisting every temptation to reject them too. It is your mature and non-vindictive attitude that will turn their rejection into acceptance.

What Snares are You Likely to Encounter in this Phase?

The worst trap in this season is revenge, the desire to hit back and retaliate against those who have treated you unjustly and sought to abort your servanthood. Another trap is to be completely overwhelmed, crushed by the rejection to such a degree that you become totally disillusioned. This will neutralise and immobilise your servanthood. At the worst, it will cause you to walk away from your servanthood.

What Lessons Should a Servant Take Away from this Season?

"Most fears of rejection rest on the desire for approval from other people. Don't base your self-esteem on their opinions." (Harvey Mackay)

Every season of rejection gives you an opportunity for a period of reflection, so take time to remember the following:

- That being rejected and isolated is an opportunity to take time to know yourself, reflect and take stock
- That being rejected and isolated is a way of being separated and hidden so that growth in character can be accomplished
- That being rejected reveals to a servant what they are made of, including your capacity to survive and even thrive in adverse circumstances
- That your joy is not in the hands of other people but in your own hands

How to Time Your Transition from this Season

You will know this season is coming to an end when you learn the lessons you were meant to learn, and when you have demonstrated your maturity to your leader and co-workers. When your leader and co-workers begin to accept and embrace you, then you know that the season is ending and the time for advancing has begun.

"Rejection gives you more power to push forward" (Jeremy Limn).

Blessed are you when men hate you, and when they exclude you, and revile you, and cast out your name as evil, for the Son of Man's sake. Rejoice in that day and leap for joy! For indeed your reward is great in heaven, for in like manner their fathers did to the prophets. (Luke 6:22-23)

3. THE SEASON OF EXPLOITATION

What is the nature of this season?

This is a season in which a leader oppresses their servant by taking advantage of them, treating them unfairly in order to benefit from the servant's labour. This kind of exploitation can come in many forms, for example in refusing to pay wages or compensations.

What is the purpose of this season and what lessons should a servant take away from this season?

There are different ways in which the exploited servant can benefit from such a season:

- The servant discovers gifts and talents that they did not know existed
- The servant is provoked to become proactive rather than just reactive, to show initiative and display innovation
- The servant learns endurance and perseverance

- The servant can rest in the knowledge that this is just a season
- The servant can acquire wisdom for strategizing their exit from this season
- The servant can learn that if they respond rightly, they will not exit this season empty-handed

How to be positioned in this season

Clothe your mind with the following garments, which are positive attitudes, knowing that you position yourself

- By applying self-control and restraint
- By not murmuring and complaining
- By using wisdom, hard work and strategizing to survive and thrive in the season
- By focusing on your mission and servanthood
- By remaining submitted and fruitful

How to relate appropriately to the different people you'll encounter in this season

The first kind of person you will often encounter in this season is the Laban-like leader. You relate to them by developing wisdom, strategies and skills to outsmart them without displaying any hostility or disrespect.

The second type of person is your fellow servants who are not themselves being exploited because the Laban-like leader has strong emotional ties to them. Since you also have strong emotional ties to this Laban figure, they may not even be aware that you are being exploited. Even if they are, they have no power to help you because their loyalties are conflicted between you and the leader. Your response is to understand them and avoid involving them in your plans and strategies.

What Snares are You Likely to Encounter in this Phase?

- The temptation to engage in evil and wrongdoing towards your Laban as an act of revenge. This will leave you as the loser.
- The temptation to force your fellow workers to choose between being loyal to you or to Laban. In this case you will again be the loser.
- The temptation to become bitter, angry and offended so that you do not acquire any wisdom, skills and strategies that God wanted you to discover and develop in that season. Again, you end up losing and missing your promotion.

What Lessons Should a Servant Takeaway from this Season?

You learn how to thrive in adversity by acquiring wisdom, skills and strategy. You learn how not to rock the boat, how to avoid becoming aggressive and confrontational in situations where you do not have enough bargaining power.

How to Time Your Transition from this Season

You will know this season has come to an end when you have accumulated enough strength, wisdom and skills to separate from your Laban. You will also know when you have no more grace to remain and you realise that any confrontation with your Laban will leave you the loser, so you choose to exit peacefully.

4.   THE SEASON OF PURGING AND THRESHING

"As threshing separates the wheat from the chaff, so does affliction purify virtue." (Christian Nestell Bovee)

What is the Nature of the Season?

This is a season when a servant undergoes various wildernesses such as sickness, affliction, severe financial lack, extreme stress and broken relationships. It is a time when seemingly anything and everything that could go wrong, does go wrong.

What is the Purpose of this Season?

"Purge everything that's holding you back. Whatever it is you feel you are being deprived of, trust the limitation serves to bring you more of what you want." *(Holly Lynn Payne)*

The purpose of this season is

- To smooth out your rough edges
- To panel beat and mould your character
- To sift the wheat from the chaff
- To remove the dross from the silver in the refiner's fire
- To mature you into a vessel of honour, tested and found equipped to serve effectively
- To remove anything in you that may hinder you from being effective in servanthood

How to be Positioned in this Season

You position yourself for maximum benefit in this season

- By succumbing to the fiery furnace and allowing the refiner's fire to cleanse and purify you from any pride or stubbornness.
- By surrendering to the threshing floor and allowing the sifting of your character so that anything that needs to be removed can be shaken off your life.

How to relate appropriately to the different people you'll encounter in this season

There are two kinds of character you will encounter:

1. Your Leader

Someone in authority in your life will be the one appointed and ordained to carry out the purging and threshing. They will do this through the way they handle and treat you. See this as a form of preparation for true servanthood. Embrace the purging and threshing, knowing it is for your good.

2. Your Co-Workers

You will not usually go through this alone. Often there are those being threshed with you. Some cannot handle the threshing and they perish in the process and abort their servanthood. You relate to these people with compassion and not judgement because your strength is not their strength. Others can handle it like you, so you comfort and encourage one another in your common sufferings.

What Snares are You Likely to Encounter in this Phase?

One snare is to react negatively against your thresher and purger, thereby missing the valuable preparation they were ordained to impart to you. By turning your back on them, you turn down the opportunity to be moulded into the invaluable character of a true servant. You will then remain mediocre without ever excelling.

What Lessons Should a Servant Take away from This Season?

You must come to understand that you have been carrying excess baggage, dross and chaff in your character and that this needed to be recognised and removed. You must also come to see that being called to servanthood is one step, but preparation and formation are vital too if you are to become effective and successful in your servanthood.

How to Time Your Transition from this Season

You will know that the threshing and purging has come to an end

- When you no longer feel the pain of this process
- When you reach a point of enjoying your growth and development because you have understood its value
- When you sense a new maturity in your character
- When you overcome and have victory over issues and attitudes within you that you previously struggled with

"Commit. Purge. Replenish." (James Smythe)

5.   THE SEASON OF INTENSE BATTLE AND WARFARE

What is the nature of this season?

This is a time when the leader and vision come under vicious attacks from shakings, scandals, false accusations, afflictions or even sickness. As a servant, you will find yourself in a deep and intense mode of firefighting and damage control if you are to shield and protect your leader and their vision.

What is the Purpose of this Season?

- To test the leader's heart and commitment to the vision
- To test the servant's loyalty and commitment to their servanthood
- To shake the servant out of their comfort zone, the place of slumber

How to be positioned in this season

- By obeying the call to prayer
- By engaging in intercession and warfare
- By becoming extremely alert to danger
- By drawing on all the wisdom and strategies of defence that you have learned over the years

- By remaining calm, not allowing panic and fear to take hold of you, because you must remain a strength and pillar to your leader

How to relate appropriately to the different people you'll encounter in this season

1. External Enemies
   Respond by using the weapons within you
2. Your Leader
   Respond by shielding and protecting them
3. Your Co-Servants
   Respond by supporting, encouraging and edifying one another

What Snares are You Likely to Encounter in this Phase?

- The temptation to panic during battle, forgetting that you have powerful weapons at your disposal, allowing the enemy to conquer you
- The temptation to betray your leader and co-workers and to join the enemy because your adversary appears stronger

What Lessons Should a Servant Take Away from this Season?

- That your purpose and calling involves confronting an enemy who will constantly seek to oppose and destroy you.
- That you are more powerful than you think you are and that there are weapons within you at your disposal.
- That once you are rooted in your right call and purpose, once you are located within your right place of servanthood, no enemy can defeat you.
- That the leader, people and vision you are serving are precious treasures that the enemy will seek to destroy, and it is your duty to value and protect them

How to time your transition from this season

You will know the season has come to an end when your enemy retreats and you have the victory.

"In every battle there comes a time when both sides consider themselves beaten, then he who continues the attack wins" (Ulysses S. Grant).

Ecclesiastes 3:1 says, *"To everything there is a season. A time for every purpose under heaven."*

You will know it is over when the enemy retreats and there is a rest from warfare.

6.   THE SEASON OF REST TO REPLENISH

"There is virtue in work and there is virtue in rest. Use both and overlook neither." (Alan Cohen)

What is the nature of this season?

It is a season to step back from active servanthood. It is a time when the servant is removed from their place of servanthood, maybe because the servant is sick or tired.

What is the purpose of this season?

- To experience self-growth
- To sharpen your sense of who you are
- To restore your spirit, soul and body
- To rest, replenish, renew, rejuvenate
- To restock and take stock
- To evaluate, analyse, reflect, measure milestones and missed opportunities

How to be positioned in this season

Clothe your mind with the following attitudes and actions:

- Relax –be still
- Surrender-let go
- Realize you are not indispensable
- Remember that you are human, not superhuman
- Believe that in your absence, others are capable
- Learn how to delegate effectively
- Purpose to respect your mind and body

"To be at rest is to be at peace." (Lailah Gifty Akita)

How to relate appropriately to the different people you'll encounter in this season

A good leader will encourage you to rest despite your resistance. Respond to them by obeying the call to rest the same way you obey the call to work. Then there will be those who will try to convince you that you do not need to rest and who will also accuse you of laziness. Ignore them and proceed to your place of rest because you don't owe them an explanation and it is not your responsibility to make them understand.

"Rest is not idleness, and to lie sometimes on the grass under trees on a summer's day, listening to the murmur of the water, or watching the clouds float across the sky, is by no means a waste of time." (John Lubbock)

What Snares are You Likely to Encounter in this Phase?

The first pitfall is your own stubborn resistance to rest. By resisting, you will end up burned out and useless for servanthood. The second pitfall is the temptation to rest excessively, to continue in rest mode even after the season has expired. Do not stay in your comfort zone, refusing to return to your servanthood. Rest with the intention of replenishment, but then return to your servanthood.

What lessons should a servant take away from this season?

You learn that you are a mere mortal and that you cannot serve with an unhealthy, exhausted body, and that you are not indispensable and that, in your absence, there are others equally able to do what you do.

How to Time Your Transition from this Season

It is time to get back to servanthood when you begin to feel rejuvenated, revived and excited about returning to your servanthood, and when your mind becomes alert with fresh ideas and strategies which you were unable to conceive before because you were too tired. Remember, the richest revelations are discovered in the sweetest rest.

7. THE SEASON OF PROMOTION

"It is only the farmer who faithfully plants seed in the Spring and who reaps a harvest in the Autumn." (B. C. Forbes)

What is the nature of the season?

This is a season of moving to the next level of responsibility and servanthood because the servant has mastered the current level. It is a season for you to reap what you have sown.

What is the Purpose of this Season?

- To upgrade
- To shift to a new level
- To prove you have the capacity for a new level
- To demonstrate your growth as a servant
- To demonstrate that you have matured

"I determine to render more and better servanthood, each day, than I am being paid to render. Those that reach the top are the ones who are not content with doing only what is required of them." *(Og Mandino)*

How to be positioned in this season

Clothe your mind with the following attitudes:

- I will accept new levels without any apologies
- I will enjoy the rewards of promotion
- I will understand that with new privileges come great responsibilities
- I will be alert and vigilant because new levels cause new devils to manifest

How to Relate Appropriately to the Different People You'll Encounter in this Season

To the leader who is promoting you because you have been a good and faithful servant, respond with gratitude and humility. With your fellow servants who are being promoted, celebrate. With your co-servants who have not yet been promoted, be humble and encourage them without pride or mockery.

What Snares are You Likely to Encounter in this Phase?

- The temptation to be proud and self-righteous about your achievements
- The temptation to believe the lie that you got there by yourself
- The temptation to mock those who are not being promoted
- The temptation to forget to be grateful and to acknowledge those who helped you get to your place of promotion

What lessons should a servant take away from this season?

- That good servanthood and hard work pays and that your labour of love is never in vain
- That excelling and commitment have rewards
- That there are new levels in servanthood
- That despite the pit, Potiphar and the prison, the palace is guaranteed if you remain faithful, committed and patient as Joseph was (Genesis 37, 39)
- That faithful servanthood leads to your 'Boaz' and to your double portion *(The Book of Ruth)*
- That there is a Boaz for every faithful Ruth, and a double portion
- That there is a mountain to inherit for every faithful Caleb
- That there is a ceremony of celebration for every Mordecai *(The Book of Esther)*

How to Time Your Transition from This Season

"The law of harvest is to reap more than you sow." (James Allen)

This season will have come to an end when you need to apply and prove yourself at a new level of authority and the cycle of seasons begins again.

Thought Provoking Questions for Discussion

1. During your season of persecution, what was your greatest challenge and breaking point and how did you stop yourself from going over the edge?

2. During your season of rejection, what was your greatest challenge and breaking point and how did you stop yourself from going over the edge?

3. During your season of exploitation, what was your greatest challenge and breaking point and how did you stop yourself from going over the edge?

4. During your season of purging and threshing, what was your greatest challenge and breaking point and how did you stop yourself from going over the edge?

5. During your season of intense battle and attacks, what was your greatest challenge and breaking point and how did you stop yourself from going over the edge?

6. During your season of rest and replenishment, what was your greatest challenge and how did you stop yourself from going over the edge?

7. During your season of promotion and harvest, what was your greatest challenge and how did you stop yourself from going over the edge?

THE 7 SHARP SURGERIES OF SERVANTHOOD

If you are to serve effectively, you must have every part of your being in optimum working condition. In this section we are going to be looking at your eyes, mind, ears, mouth, nose, heart, hands, knees and feet as symbols of various functions of your servanthood. They are fundamental to your ability to serve well.

Each of these aspects of a servant's life will require a metaphorical form of surgery from time to time if they are to be fit and healthy for active service. Each one must be whole because together they are interdependent. When one is defective, all are affected.

How a servant uses these functions will determine the effectiveness of their servanthood. It may even make or break them.

A sensitive servant will know which aspect is wanting or defective and they will be open to having it healed and refined, so that they can serve effectively.

In The Book of Leviticus 21:18-22, we see how no one was allowed to serve at the altar if they were blind or had any eye defects (symbolizing lack of or impaired vision), a flat nose (symbolizing the inability to perceive or discern divine revelation), was lame, crippled or paralysed (symbolizing an inability to function) or even disfigured with deformed feet or hands (symbolizing an inability to work). A dwarf or a hunchback (symbolizing lack of uprightness or honesty) were also not supposed to serve at the altar, nor anyone with any skin disease. These disabilities can be used as symbols of spiritual, ethical or moral shortcomings that hamper and hinder effective servanthood.

As we examine the required procedure needed in each case, we must remember that the word "surgery" denotes the treatment of a disorder by either cutting something out or off - or making incisions in order to remove or correct something. In this context, it means cutting and removing things from our lives such as negative traits and habits, toxic relationships, past pain, distractive patterns of behaviour, limiting beliefs, hindrances, unhealthy emotions and attitudes and chronic recurring problems.

For a servant to be effective, they therefore need to submit to the surgeon's knife at certain seasons of their lives. They must be prepared to undergo processes and procedures of radical refining in which the various aspects of their lives – symbolized by the mind, eyes, feet etc – are examined and then corrected where needed.

In the following, we look at seven key areas of servanthood that need to be healthy and fit if a servant is to operate at the highest level of efficiency and efficacy.

The 7 Sevens

1. **THE MIND (THE REFINING OF A SERVANT'S THOUGHT PATTERNS)**

What do we mean by the mind and what does it symbolize?

The word "mind" refers to your established set of attitudes, thought patterns, and assumptions. The word "mind" is a symbol for your "mind-set".

What is a Defective Mind-set in a Servant?

If you have fixed thoughts and attitudes towards situations, you can end up stubbornly refusing to change or adjust. This inflexibility is a sign of an unhealthy mind-set. This leads to wrong actions because what you believe affects how you behave. A defective mind-set is caused by fixating on problems as negative realties instead of as opportunities. People with negative thinking and limiting beliefs see the worst in everything.

What Surgery is Required?

A servant with an unhealthy, fixed mentality will need radical surgery to reframe their mind-set into one that grows and adjusts, one that is positive not negative.

How to Heal a Defective Mind-set

a) Allow yourself to open your mind and let it be flexible. *"Mind is a flexible mirror. Adjust it to see a better world"* (***Amit Ray***). ***A fixed mind-set can be changed***
b) Develop the right beliefs and a positive attitude
c) Associate with happy people with positive attitudes. ***"Happiness depends on your mind-set and attitude" (Roy T. Bennett)***
d) Examine your beliefs regularly and erase self-limiting, self-sabotaging thoughts.
"Once your mind-set changes, everything on the outside will change along with it" (Steve Maraboli).
e) Sieve your thoughts and guard and protect your mind. Effective servanthood will require you to have a healthy, growth-oriented mind set.

A Healed Mindset

Once the mind of a servant has undergone radical surgery, they will have a totally different mind-set characterised by the following:

- They will have positive thoughts and attitudes
- They will see opportunities where they previously saw problems
- They will operate in a more enthusiastic manner
- Their mind will be open to new ideas and concepts
- They will be more positive in relating to people
- They will be more confident in responding to challenges and obstacles

2. THE EYES (THE REFINING OF A SERVANT'S VISION AND FORESIGHT)

What is the Eye and What Does it Symbolize?

Eyes symbolize a person's vision, their ability to perceive and see sharply. It is a tragic thing to have physical eyesight without inner vision. The eyes point to our ability to dream dreams, to conceive of and pursue ideas. How and what a servant sees will determine the quality and effectiveness of their servanthood. Their perspective of people and situations will need to be correct otherwise they will fall into errors of judgement and be guilty of operating with prejudicial thinking. A servant's vision must therefore be powerful, long and clear. They need to be able to see things and situations in a far-reaching and deep way, beyond the superficial and shallow level with which others operate. They must have 20/20 vision, with eyes that are not blurred or clouded by biases.

What are Defective Eyes in a Servant?

Infection

This symbolizes external contamination from seeing defiled things and from focusing on the evil in the world.

Allergy

Allergies can cause distortion of vision. When their eyesight is clouded by misconceptions and biases (the equivalent of allergic reactions), a servant's vision becomes warped and limited. Blurred vision leads to wrong conclusions and skewed judgements.

Poor diet

Lack of proper diet and rest causes poor eyesight. A good servant will constantly monitor what they are feeding off intellectually, spiritually, morally, emotionally – at every level of their personhood and being.

What Surgery is Required?

The following may be required:

- To remove "cataracts" - the unhealed issues that cloud the servant's vision.
- To rectify "short-sightedness" which hinders a servant from seeing fine details, thereby missing crucial information in decision making.
- To rectify "longsightedness" so that they can see far ahead and be a visionary.

Healed Eyes

Once your eyes have undergone radical surgery, you will experience the following benefits:

- You will see issues sharply and clearly
- You will be able to have foresight in respect of the vision and goals
- You will be able to scrutinize and discriminate issues more competently and you will be able to see people and issues from a more accurate perspective
- You will see and view yourself more accurately, no longer despising yourself because of limited insight
- Like an eagle you will be able to see your enemies from afar and warn of oncoming dangers like storms.

3. THE EARS (THE REFINING OF A SERVANT'S HEARING)

What are the Ears and What Do They Symbolize?

A servant's ability to hear clearly and accurately is crucial because they need to hear instructions well if they are to implement and execute them. They must learn to hear even the unspoken, so their ears must be clear. A servant's hearing is closely allied with their obedience because you cannot obey properly and fully that which you have not heard properly and fully.

"The greatest problem with communication is we don't listen to understand. We listen to reply. When we listen with curiosity, we don't listen with intent to reply. We listen for what's behind the words" (Roy T Bennett).

What are defective ears?

Defective ears will cause a servant not to hear instructions properly, or to imagine what they are hearing, or to deflect what they are hearing, or to project their own understanding onto what they are hearing. When their ears are blocked because of listening to negative talk and gossip (wax in the inner ear), that clogging hinders them from hearing the right things.

Furthermore, a servant's ears may become infected because of carelessness – for example, inserting dangerous objects into their ears. This damages the eardrum and prevents them from hearing properly. Think of these objects as dangerous information and propaganda designed to derail you from the right path in your servanthood. This becomes audible when you associate with people who are either enemies to your leader and the vision, or who pretend to be behind your leader but are not. It can come from mixing with people who are neither for or against your leader and who simply do not care. Avoid being in places where defamatory and negative reports are spoken about your leader. When you are in such unhelpful environments, your ears can become defiled and defective. Once you hear negative information about your leader, it is hard to erase it from your memory.

What Surgery is Required?

The following kinds of drastic, metaphorical procedures may be necessary at certain times in your servanthood if you are to have healthy ears:

- Radically rejecting every piece of negative information and talk that you have allowed to infect and afflict your ears. This can only be done by listening to that which is pure, true, sincere, motivational, uplifting and edifying to replace the contamination.
- Radically cutting every association in your life that causes you to listen to dirt, filth, falsity and negativity especially about your leader and the vision.
- Purposefully and intentionally sieving and selecting what you allow yourself to hear and the company you choose to keep

This process will, of course, be painful because it may mean losing or lessening relationships and refraining from going to places and engaging in activities that give you pleasure.

Healed Ears

A servant with healed ears will develop empathetic listening. Stephen Covey has outlined what this looks like in *The 7 Habits Of Highly Effective People*. Empathetic listening means to seek first to understand what the other person is saying before you seek to be understood. It means listening with the intent to understand how the speaker is feeling and understanding his or her ideas. A servant who develops empathetic listening identifies with another person's emotions and situations even if they may not agree with them. Once they have been through this kind of aural surgery, the servant will develop empathetic listening which is the highest form of hearing.

4. THE MOUTH (THE REFINING OF A SERVANT'S WORDS OR SPEECH)

"Remember not only to say the right thing in the right place, but far more difficult still, to leave unsaid the wrong thing at the tempting moment." (Benjamin Franklin)

What is the Mouth and What Does it Symbolize?

It symbolizes speech. A servant's words and speech will need to be refined if they are to represent their leader accurately and effectively. A servant with a defective mouth is like a Judas who is ready to betray his leader.

What does a Defective Mouth Look Like?

1. The Content

This refers to *what* you say. When it is unhealthy (careless talk, gossip, slander, unfiltered words), it causes halitosis. Foul breath is a symbol of unwholesome, and hurtful talk.

2. The Environment

This refers more to the *where* than the what. Too much time in the wrong context with the wrong people will cause you to start speaking the wrong things.

3. The Timing

This refers to *when* one talks. Saying the wrong thing at the wrong time, or saying the right thing at the wrong time, is a sign of a defective mouth.

4. The Motivation

This refers to *why* you speak. If your intention is to utter words that are destructive to your leader then that is an example of a defective mouth.

"Let's acknowledge the difference between speaking up with intention and speaking up for attention" (Monica Lewinsky).

5. The recipients

This refers to who you talk to. If you speak to the wrong people, or in the presence of the wrong people, your words may disclose too much or become twisted by others.

6. The Attitude

This refers to how one talks - the tone, volume, body language and facial expression. Proverbs 18:21 says, *"Death and life are in the power of the tongue, and those who love it will eat its fruit."* Those who speak words of death have defective mouths.

What Surgery is Required?

- Scrape out all foul talk and speech with the sword of the Word of God. Use your mouth to read and speak words that edify
- Rinse your mouth with prayer, praise and worship, with pure, sincere, relevant talk seasoned with truth and grace in order to eradicate bad breath
- Inundate your heart with grace, peace, patience, and

kindness because your mouth speaks from the abundance of your heart

- Constantly feed your mind with instructions about where to speak and where not to speak
- Focus on the power of good timing as well as on the dangers of wrong timing
- Let your heart guard your mouth as regards its motives
- Discriminately sieve who you associate with and guard who you talk to
- Purify your lips like Isaiah the prophet as a reminder to speak only that which is right and pure
- Remove yourself from people of unclean lips to prevent their evil speech flowing from your mouth like effluent.

A Healed Mouth

A healed mouth is a powerful and useful tool and weapon in the hands of a faithful servant. After the mouth has undergone radical surgery, you will learn to be a person of few words and you will start to listen more and talk less.

"A good speech should be like a woman's skirt; long enough to cover the subject and short enough to create interest" (Winston S. Churchill).

A healed mouth will utter words that are seasoned with grace and wisdom. A healed mouth will consult with the mind and think carefully before talking. A servant with a healed mouth can be trusted to remain confidential and to guard the welfare of their leader from betrayal and sabotage.

5. THE HEART (THE REFINING OF A SERVANT'S EMOTIONS)

What is the Heart and What Does it Symbolize?

The heart symbolizes your emotions and feelings. A servant's heart must be pure and healthy for effective servanthood. The heart bears both positive and negative burdens, agendas, motives and emotions. The condition of your heart is crucial because it affects and determines what comes out of your mouth.

What is a Defective Heart?

The heart can become sick and defiled due to the following:

- Unforgiveness towards those who have wronged you
- Bitterness, jealousy and envy, for example, a resentment that co-workers have been promoted and you have not
- Anger and offence
- Hurt from past pain
- Disappointments and frustrations arising from feelings of not being appreciated or receiving the rewards or successes you expected
- Self-pity and a victim syndrome
- Selfish ambitions, motives and agendas, seeking your own interests before the interests of your leader and others.
- Hatred caused by your mistrust of people and your inability to develop healthy relationships during your servanthood.

What Surgery is Required?

If your heart is to become fit and healthy again, there are things that others can do for you (the surgeon) and there are things you can do for yourself (exercise, good diet, etc). In terms of the latter, here are some healthy things you should do:

- Humble yourself and acknowledge that you are harbouring these issues in your heart.
- Put your pride and harshness aside and address and confront each issue radically, cutting and uprooting them from your heart.
- Replace all negative and toxic issues with their antidotes - forgiveness, love, patience, kindness and forbearance

A Healed Heart

Once the heart has undergone radical surgery, you will do the following:

- Harbour sincere and selfless motives
- Forgive easily and show kindness, patience, love and tolerance
- Develop and maintain healthier relationships
- Experience greater passion and enthusiasm in your servanthood
- Create a shield against negative emotions by surrounding yourself with positive people
- Keep your heart filled with positive feelings.

"A man sees in the world what he carries in his heart" (Johann Wolfgang von Goethe).

6. THE HANDS (THE REFINING OF A SERVANT'S ACTIONS)

What are the hands and what do they symbolize?

Hands symbolise work, diligence, ethical action.

What are Defective Hands in a Servant?

1) Broken Hands

The hands of a person who has become fractured by hurts

2) Lazy Hands

The hands of a person with a deficient work ethic and an unwillingness to work hard

3) Weak Hands

The hands of a person who procrastinates and who debilitates their team

4) Defiled Hands

The hands of someone who has been in contact with corruption

5) Heavy Hands

The heavy-handedness of someone who misuses power, lording it over people

What Surgery is Required?

- Fix the broken hands
- Strengthen the weak hands
- Empower the lazy hands
- Cleanse the defiled hands
- Confront the heavy hands

Healed Hands

Once you have been healed, you will have stronger hands and be more productive and fruitful, set free from laziness and lethargy. You will operate with the right values and good work ethics. You will develop self-motivation and an increased energy. You will develop temperance and moderation in handling people instead of being heavy-handed.

How to maintain healthy hands

- Develop good work ethics
- Develop core values
- Develop self-motivation –
  "In order to obtain and hold power, a man must love it."
  (Leo Tolstoy)
- Develop purity -Psalm 24:3-4, *Who may ascend into the hill of the Lord? Or who may stand in His holy place? He who has clean hands and a pure heart, Who has not lifted up his soul to an idol, nor sworn deceitfully.*

7.   THE FEET (THE REFINING OF A SERVANT'S WALK)

"When God calls a man to be upright and pure and generous, he also calls him to be intelligent and skilful, and strong and brave."
(Orison Swett Marden)

What are the Feet and What Do They Symbolize?

Feet symbolise your walk, lifestyle, values, ethics, principles, your ability to move forward and to pass milestones. As a servant, you need to have healthy feet because feet symbolize your obedience in going where you are sent. Feet also symbolize your ability to be stable and grounded in your place of servanthood. They point to your walk and lifestyle in terms of your morals and character. The washing of feet symbolizes servanthood as Jesus taught. The feet also symbolize possessing and taking authority over territories and situations.

What are Defective Feet?

This is when as a servant your walk and lifestyle are questionable in terms of your honesty and integrity.

Defective feet can be:

1) Lame Feet

This can be something you inherit or something you invite. Either way, this ends up with you exhibiting a walk picked up from your family and ancestry. A dishonest walk may derive from dishonesty in the way your forefathers walked or from your own choices. Walking uprightly means living with good morals and with integrity.

2) Crippled Feet

Feet can become crippled through accidents. This is symbolic of the fact that although you do not intentionally choose to have a defective walk, nonetheless there are unconscious choices you make that hamper you greatly from moving forward. Although you are serving, you are serving with difficulty and therefore not effectively.

3) Heavyset Feet

Having heavyset feet makes you slow. This can occur either because you are wearing the wrong kinds of shoes or because you have failed to take enough exercise. This greatly hampers your movement. This wrong footwear symbolizes lack of proper understanding and information, leading to the lack of proper equipment and tools required in your servanthood. The lack of exercise symbolizes a lack of proper habits (such as self-discipline) which will make your servanthood light and expeditious.

4) Cold Feet

These symbolize a lack of courage, being indecisive and procrastinating in your walk and lifestyle, thereby greatly handicapping yourself from effective servanthood. Cold feet suggest someone who has an unstable mind - a mind that changes hastily and carelessly.

What Surgery is Required?

Lame feet will need to be given braces and realigned. This kind of servant will need to be given the required support in terms of accountable relationships and will need to be coached into believing in and modelling good work ethics.

Crippled feet will need correction, replacing the disability with ability. You will need to address radically your wrong actions, choices and habits so that your walk and lifestyle can be corrected – i.e. enabled and empowered as opposed to being disabled.

Heavyset feet will need to be unburdened and lightened in order for you to acquire a swiftness and speed in adopting right habits, empowering yourself with understanding and knowledge as regards your servanthood, resulting in you being able to serve expeditiously and energetically.

Cold feet will need warming up and this will require you to develop greater self-confidence through a securer sense of identity and self-worth, leading to the kind of courage that enables you to be proactive in making your decisions and consistent in your thinking.

Healed Feet

Once your feet (walk and lifestyle) have undergone a radical surgery, you will develop good morals and good values. You will become accountable as regards your lifestyle, walk and servanthood. Your commitment will be restored, and you will develop an ability to go to the right places at the right time. You will develop obedience in your servanthood and go where you are sent. You will walk uprightly with integrity and truth without being bent over and crippled – i.e., compromising and being economical with the truth.

You will become solidly grounded in your place of servanthood. You will wear the right footwear (having the right equipment, understanding and tools for your assignment).

Uphold my steps in Your paths, that my footsteps may not slip. (Psalms 17:5)

Oh, continue Your loving kindness to those who know You, and Your righteousness to the upright in heart. Let not the foot of pride come against me and let not the hand of the wicked drive me away (Psalms 36:10-11)

"We never know the journey another person has walked, so be kind to everyone." (Lynette Mather)

Conclusion

The above list of aspects of the human mind and body is by no means exhaustive. For example, sometimes we may need radical surgery in the womb to uproot Ishmaels (misconceived visions and dreams and seed ideas) planted through our own carnality or by the enemy. Our knees may also need surgery where they have become rigid through lack of bending in prayer, where we have adopted attitudes of pride and rebellion. The list, in other words, is not final and comprehensive. However, I have included enough to indicate the importance of the servant being healthy and fit at every level. The effective servant is one who is committed to keeping every part of their being as healthy as possible, knowing their servanthood is a marathon, not a sprint.

Thought Provoking Questions for Discussion

1. During the radical surgery of your mind, what aspects of your mind had the greatest defects and what was the greatest benefit you saw after the surgery?

2. During the radical surgery of your eyes, what aspects of your eyes had the greatest defects and what was the greatest benefit you saw after the surgery?

3. During the radical surgery of your ears, what aspects of your ears had the greatest defects and what was the greatest benefit you saw after the surgery?

4. During the radical surgery of your mouth, what aspects of your mouth had the greatest defects and what was the greatest benefit you saw after the surgery?

5. During the radical surgery of your heart, what aspects of your heart had the greatest defects and what was the greatest benefit you saw after the surgery?

6. During the radical surgery of your hands, what aspects of your hands had the greatest defects and what was the greatest benefit you saw after the surgery?

7. During the radical surgery of your feet, what aspects of your feet had the greatest defects and what was the greatest benefit you saw after the surgery?

This Page Was Intentionally Left Blank

Chapter 7

THE PRIZE
OF FAITHFUL
SERVANTHOOD

*Laying Hold of the Rewards of Your Faithful
Servanthood*

***"There is no limit as to how much man can do
as long as he doesn't care who gets the glory."* ~
Nelson Mandela**

Chapter Outline

The 7 External Rewards

1. Promotion to Higher Positions

2. Inheritance of Material Substance

3. Corporate Benefits

4. Honorarium

5. God's Favour, Presence and Protection

6. Succession to Leadership

7. Good Success for Good Servanthood

The 7 Internal Rewards

1. Honour and Esteem

2. Double Portion Empowerment

3. Personal Joy and Fulfilment

4. A Desired Harvest

5. Recognition

6. Legacy

7. Fulfilment of God's Agenda

The 7 Eternal Rewards

1. Mansions In Heaven

2. Crowns

3. Eternal Life

4. Praise

5. God As a Reward

6. Protection

7. Escaping Tribulation

INTRODUCTION

After paying the price of faithful servanthood, you will receive rewards. This chapter on rewards is the shortest, not because rewards are not important but because the rewards should never be your primary focus.

"Your rewards in life are in direct proportion to your service" (Earl Nightingale).

A good servant will thrive, blossom and flourish wherever they are planted despite all the challenges. The sacrifices and pain of servanthood are never in vain and a faithful servant must remain motivated by the incentives of servanthood.

"The greatest rewards only come from the greatest committed" (Arlene Blum).

As the Apostle Paul wrote in Philippians 3:14: *"I press towards the goal for the prize of the upward call of God in Christ Jesus."*

A true servant does not chase after accolades and recognition but maintains a low profile. They serve in the background, allowing their leader to shine and take the credit. While this happens, a faithful servant is patient and full of faith, knowing that there are rewards from God that cannot compare with any rewards from man. As Romans 2:6 says: *"He will render to each one according to his deeds."*

And as Rulph Ransom comments,

"Before the reward there must be labour. You plant before you harvest. Your sow in tears before you reap in joy."

The rewards of your servanthood will be external and extrinsic, internal and intrinsic, or eternal and heavenly. Often it is a combination of all three. Your rewards will be continuous in the journey of your servanthood but there will also be other rewards that you will receive at the end of your service. The key is to remain motivated and faithful, certain that your rewards are guaranteed. As Colossians 3:23-24 says,

"Whatever you do, do it heartily as to the Lord and not to men, knowing that from the Lord you will receive the reward of the inheritance for you serve the Lord Christ."

Someone has said, *"It is the things we work hardest for that will reward us the most."*

As you lay hold of the prize - the harvest and the rewards for your faithful service - you will notice that they these benefits impact all areas of your life: your personal health, the health of your loved ones, your finances and business, your relationships, your career and calling, your visions and goals, and so forth. It is important that you take time to understand the nature and the truths about your rewards, the reasons why you're receiving them, the right ways to respond to your rewards, and the hindrances and threats that will come against your rewards and how to overcome them. This antagonism is because your rewards may sometimes be threatened by the tares or weeds that you need to watch and then uproot so that your harvest is not compromised.

These tares may include **(a)** a sense of egotistical pride in the success of your servanthood, **(b)** a belief that the harvest is solely down to you, leaving you unwilling to share your rewards with those around you who assisted you on the way, or **(c)** a sense of entitlement which leads you to question and despise the quantity of your reward, leaving you languishing in ingratitude. Every one of these tares is a threat and you must be careful to discern the early seedlings and nip them in the bud.

You must always remember that your service is unto God through man, so the true rewards are from God provided the service aligns with God's agenda. You must also remember that the Lord honours service. As Jesus said in John12:26, *"If anyone serves Me, let him follow Me; and where I am, there My servant will be also. If anyone serves Me, him My Father will honour."*

THE 7 EXTERNAL REWARDS (EXTRINSIC)

External rewards are extrinsic in that they come from outside us. They are visible or invisible, tangible or intangible, spiritual or material. For example, the gifts of a piece of land and a building are visible, tangible, material rewards. Good will and added brand value are invisible, intangible, and more spiritual or immaterial in nature. Here are some of the extrinsic rewards for active, effective and faithful servanthood.

1. PROMOTION TO HIGHER POSITIONS

A faithful servant may be promoted to a higher position of servanthood where they have greater responsibilities, greater influence and impact, a wider jurisdiction to oversee and more material resources to steward. This gives them access to more material benefits, thereby empowering them and lifting their standard of living.

This kind of prize and reward can be received in corporate organizations, businesses and enterprises, also in churches and non-profit organizations. They can be given in any sphere, sector or industry where faithful service on your part merits being given an opportunity to exercise more authority and a greater opportunity to transform lives, a greater chance to make a difference and a greater freedom to leave a more impactful legacy. For example, you may be promoted from being a magistrate to a judge, or from the judge of a lower court to the judge of a higher court, or from a manager to a managing director, or from a legal assistant to a full legal associate, or from a pastor to a bishop.

In other spheres, such as the media, you could be promoted from being a researcher who gathers information for a news anchor to the anchor, or from being an anchor to a producer or a director. And if you are a supporting actor in the arts and entertainment sphere, you may be promoted to a leading role. In the family context, your faithfulness towards your family could place you as the head of the family after the death of a parent. Even though you may not be the oldest sibling in the family, you may be the most faithful servant of your fellow family members over a long period of time.

Promotion to higher positions increases the extent of your territory, from towns to cities, cities to regions, regions to nations, and nations to continents.

2. INHERITANCE OF MATERIAL SUBSTANCE -LAND/PROPERTY/ASSETS

A faithful servant may inherit physical land, property and assets belonging to their leader. This shows that when you are faithful in stewarding another person's portfolio, you may inherit or acquire your own.

In the family sphere, your faithfulness in serving your parents may earn you a bigger inheritance than your siblings, or the privilege of being in charge of managing the family estate, having the authority over its distribution and use because you have proved to be responsible and faithful.

It is not unheard of for home and firm owners to leave their properties and assets to a faithful driver, house manager, child minder as a sign of how much they appreciated their faithfulness. In businesses, law firms or doctor's clinics, you may find yourself inheriting the business from your boss with all its assets, properties and goodwill by virtue of your faithfulness. In addition, you may even inherit an entire institution like a school, college, or church from the owner you have been faithfully serving. Even where you may not necessarily be given the assets and properties free of charge, they may be given to you at such a reasonable cost as to make it almost feel as if they are free. Where you are not rewarded with full ownership, you may be given such access to, and use of, those assets and properties to lift you up materially.

3. CORPORATE BENEFITS

This is where a faithful servant in an organization is rewarded with perks such as air tickets, a life pension, and access to company facilities. Many corporate organizations, multinationals, and public/private enterprises will have a policy for rewarding long and faithful service so that after you retire, or leave the company in good standing, there will be awards and benefits. For example, airlines have a policy whereby upon leaving you are entitled to air tickets for you and your family for life. In the case of a law firm, your faithfulness upon leaving may entitle you to free professional services for you and your family. So then, the rewards of your faithful service are continuous. This can apply to generous salary increments for good performance, bonuses, medical and other benefits including the opportunity to have your children educated and their medical needs taken care of by your employer. Such benefits are not a legal entitlement but a reward for your faithfulness.

4. HONORARIUM

A faithful servant may receive a one-off mega-monetary gift which they can invest and then live comfortably on for rest of their life. Such an honorarium can be a payment given for professional services rendered nominally, without charge. This can also be called an emolument or ex gratia payment, meaning that there is no legal obligation attached. It is a recognition that you are very valuable, with an excellent track record of faithfulness in your area of strength and expertise, and that you have offered services faithfully over a long period of time to a group of people, society or nation, either voluntarily or for a nominal fee. Receiving such an honour means that you have come to a place where you are recognized as an authority over a specific area, so much so that when you give input it is rewarded generously. The longer and more faithfully you have served, the greater the honorarium will be, even just for making an appearance at an event or function.

5. GOD'S FAVOUR, PRESENCE AND PROTECTION

A faithful servant will enjoy God's favour, protection and presence even while they are serving, not just after they have finished their service. These will in turn open many doors and provide access to unlimited material and nonmaterial rewards. These three things are interrelated; when you have one of them, you have them all.

God's favour means that you have His approval and support. Whoever you encounter will also give you approval and support, as well as resources and opportunities, that would otherwise have been difficult to access or attain. Favour means that God shows you kindness in guiding you, instructing you, cautioning you about dangers, so much so that there is tangible evidence for all to see that you are enjoying supernatural success. This favour brings promotion and then more promotion, as we can see in the case of Joseph in Genesis 29-31. Favour grants you preferential treatment, opportunities you would not have dreamt of, and acceptance by people and in places that would normally reject you. God's favour is a manifestation of His grace, which means it is unmerited. It also means God's goodwill because His pleasure is on your life, giving you favour in your relationships with kings, presidents and prime ministers, like Queen Esther. As we read in Psalm 5:12, *"For you blessed the righteous, oh Lord, and you cover him with favour as a shield."*

Now as regards God's presence, this means that God's promise to never leave you nor forsake you becomes a very real and rich revelation. You enjoy a personal encounter with God by hearing His voice clearly, understanding His instructions and cautions distinctly, being able to obey His commands easily because His presence enables you to live and walk in the Spirit, thereby silencing your flesh. God's presence empowers you with supernatural ability, comforts you in times of trouble and anxiety, and releases blessings upon you. Your prayers are heard in the presence of God and in the presence of God there is fullness of joy. As it says in Psalm 16:11, *"You will make known to me the path of life; in your presence is fullness of joy, in your right hand there are pleasures forever."*

Then with God's protection, this naturally flows from his presence and favour. God protects you from making wrong decisions even if He needs to put the proverbial donkey in your path to obstruct you! He will protect you from wrong relationships. He will thwart the evil plans of your enemies against you. He will protect you from diseases and sicknesses. He will protect whatever material substance He has blessed you with and give you wisdom to handle your prizes and rewards so that you use them well. In short, as a faithful servant who has run your race and finished well, God will ensure that His favour, protection and presence remain with you as a reward and a prize for your faithfulness. This is something you should highly prize. The absence of God's favour, presence and protection is perhaps one of the worst things that can befall us. The presence of that favour, presence and protection is what will propel you to your destiny as a faithful servant.

6. SUCCESSION TO LEADERSHIP

You cannot become an effective and fruitful leader without first having been a faithful, humble servant because good leadership is derived from good servanthood, and a good leader leads by modelling servant leadership. In view of the serious responsibility bestowed upon leaders (whether in a family, a business, a corporate organization, a multinational, a non-profit organization, a government institution, a society or even an entire nation), you need first to have been proved as a faithful servant. In the case of Joseph, his service in Potiphar's house (even though he encountered false accusations) was why he was elevated to prime minister (Genesis 39). David's faithfulness in serving King Saul had a similar effect and David's followers, who were distressed debtors, were also elevated with him.

Your training as a servant and your ability to pass all the tests, trials and tribulations of servanthood, and to finish your service faithfully, these are the things that will elevate you into leadership. The absence of these same things will hinder you from becoming a trusted and respected leader. For example, if you have served faithfully as a deputy president, you may be elevated to the president. If you have served faithfully as a deputy governor, you may be elevated to the governor. If you have served faithfully as a member of a county assembly, you may find yourself as the speaker of that assembly, and so on. A faithful servant will reap what they have sown by becoming a leader served by faithful servants. A faithful servant may often succeed their leader, with the leader handing over their organization and vision for the promoted servant to continue fulfilling it.

7. GOOD SUCCESS FOR GOOD SERVANTHOOD

God will make you successful in all your endeavours by virtue of your faithful servanthood. This success will not be fleeting either; it will stand the test of time and remain. There is a difference between good success and bad success. You may succeed in your eyes by using the wrong methods, such as dishonesty and a lack of integrity, or by undermining and wounding many people in the process. This is bad success; it leaves a trail of blood and mess. However, if you have been a faithful servant and have honoured, respected and guarded the hearts of those you were serving under, and those you were serving with, you will end up with good success as a reward.

Thought Provoking Questions for Discussion

1. Have you ever received promotion to a higher position as a reward? Did you recognize it as such?

2. In the substance of your material assets, is there something that you know for sure is the reward for your faithful servanthood?

3. Have you ever received, or do you know anyone who has received, an honorarium as a reward for faithful servanthood?

4. Have you sensed God's favour, presence and protection in your servanthood? If so, what has this looked like for you?

5. Have you ever served in an organization where you received corporate benefits as a reward? What were they and did you feel that they were adequate in proportion to your servanthood?

6. Have you ever succeeded anyone in leadership, knowing that this promotion and succession was a result for your faithful servanthood?

7. Have you experienced tangible success in areas of your life as a result of your servanthood? Which areas and what kind of success?

THE 7 INTERNAL REWARDS (INTRINSIC)

Intrinsic rewards are not physically visible, but they are extremely beneficial.

1. HONOUR AND ESTEEM

A faithful servant will be greatly honoured not only by those they have served but also by the fellow servants who admire them as a role model and a fine example of best practice. They will also be highly honoured and highly esteemed by all the beneficiaries of their service.

For example, where you have served as a teacher, trainer, coach or mentor, your students are the beneficiaries of your faithful service and for years to come they will honour and esteem you for the impact you made on their lives, the way you empowered them to excel in their various areas of strength and expertise, and the way you enabled them and propelled them to become voices in their various spheres of influence, helping them to understand their callings and life purposes, propelling them towards fulfilling their destinies. Many will honour and esteem you for having identified their gifts and talents and for having set them on the right path to discovering their right callings and careers. Had it not been for you, they might have ended up on the wrong path. Still others will honour and esteem you for having disciplined them and protected them from self-destructive lifestyles.

Parents who faithfully reared and nurtured their children to adulthood and then to the point where they become parents themselves, their children will honour and esteem them for their diligent faithfulness. If that applies to you, be heartened; in your old age, they will speak highly of you and it will bring great joy and satisfaction to your heart when your children call you blessed.

As a church leader, if you have helped your congregation to have a close relationship with God and to grow into God-fearing people, they will honour and esteem you for your tireless efforts investing in their lives.

Employers and bosses, your faithful service to the organizations and enterprises you have headed will earn you honour and respect from all those who were under you, and from all those who benefited from that organization or enterprise.

And for those in leadership and governance, whether in politics, the judiciary, security forces, legislature, civil society, civil service, the diplomatic corps or in an ambassadorial role, your faithfulness in serving and in benefiting your society and nation will be rewarded with honour and esteem.

In all the above, you become an example and a testimony when people are referring to faithful servanthood. For example, Nelson Mandela in South Africa, Michael Joseph in Safaricom Kenya, Mother Teresa in India, these are just a few of those whose names are held in great honour and esteem. Great honour is given for great service. No honour was ever simply received. It had first to be earned.

2. DOUBLE PORTION EMPOWERMENT

A faithful servant will have their gifts and talents empowered and enhanced by virtue of their loyal commitment to a leader, because they receive an impartation of the leader's giftings by the very nature of their association. Elisha knew this. He received a double portion of blessing and empowerment as a result of his faithful service to Elijah (2 Kings 2:9). This double portion of Elijah's anointing was Elisha's reward. He went on to perform twice as many miracles as Elijah had. The leader or leaders you serve have certain anointings, strengths, skills, talents, competencies, and graces which you will tap into as you serve them faithfully. After you have finished your service, and when you are elevated to become a leader, their skills, talents, competencies and graces will come upon you and you will serve at a greater measure of effectiveness and efficiency because these are added to what you already have.

In addition, any mistakes or errors of judgment your leader may have made during his leadership, you will learn from these and ensure that these are not replicated in your own leadership. That too is an empowerment of a sort. It is part of the double portion you receive as a reward for active service to that leader and their vision. This double portion reward will operate in every sphere of service.

If as a child you served your parents faithfully, the wisdom and skills within them will transfer to you when you are parenting your own children (including the wisdom not to make the same mistakes). This applies to serving a boss in any of the other spheres of society, from the eldership of a local church to the boardroom of a corporate world business. As with so many in the Bible who graduated to leadership, you will find yourself with the double portion!

3. PERSONAL JOY AND FULFILMENT

Beyond material rewards or any recognition is the personal joy and fulfilment that a servant will experience from faithful servanthood. When you see the beneficiaries of your faithful service - your students, children, employees, congregants - and when you see the benefits to the leader or leaders you are serving, how your faithful service to them has helped them to do better than they could have done had you not been faithful in your service, this brings a tremendous sense of pleasure and purpose.

There is profound fulfilment in knowing that you have touched and transformed lives and helped to shape communities, maybe even to build nations. There is fulfilment in knowing that you have been instrumental in the activation of a leader's vision that has benefited many. Personal joy and fulfilment may seem petty to some who are more interested in material rewards, but to others they are much more important than money or land because they boost self-confidence and self-esteem, giving you a sense of value in your society and nation.

4. A DESIRED HARVEST

Often when we serve, there may be a desire in our hearts for a harvest and as we remain in faithful servanthood, that desired harvest will manifest in time. For example, when Ruth was serving Naomi faithfully, her desired harvest was a Boaz. She received her harvest because she served Naomi faithfully. Likewise, we may serve desiring a harvest such as marriage, children, our own business and this is quite in order just so long as it is sincere and in line with your purpose. If it is, then that harvest will surely come as a reward for your faithful service. We should however be open to the possibility that God may have a better harvest for us than what we have desired. He knows best what we need.

Other examples of desired harvests are (a) leadership in a specific sphere, (b) certain resources for the fulfilment of your destiny, (c) specific changes in your relationships, (d) deliverance from certain forms of bondage. Whether it is something you long to receive in yourself or within others, whether it is things that you long to see on as grand scale in a much wider context - even within cultures you want to see reformed or traditions you desire to see replaced with healthier alternatives - your faithfulness as a servant will grant you the desires of your heart as a rich reward.

5. RECOGNITION

In this context we are referring to recognition in a positive sense, leading to the benefit of others, as opposed to the kind of recognition that is self-serving and leads to pride and arrogance without any benefits to others at all. To be recognized as one who has had an impact and who has made a positive influence through selfless service is a great reward. This positive recognition yields positive fruits in both you and others because it is such a good and noble example to other servants. They become motivated to be faithful in their service just as you have been. In addition, recognizing faithfulness is a mark of gratitude and appreciation, showing that people do not take your selfless service for granted. The fact that you are mature enough to receive that recognition, to use it positively as an incentive to climb to higher heights of servanthood, shows that it is positive recognition.

6. LEGACY

"Legacy is not leaving something for people. It's leaving something in people" (Peter Strople).

Everyone desires to leave a legacy for the next generation. A faithful servant who has set an example of servanthood will be remembered by the next generations as one who has left valuable footprints in the sands of time. Sometimes, as you serve faithfully, the idea of leaving a good legacy for the next generation may be the furthest thing from your mind. You may not even be conscious that your faithfulness is leaving footprints in which others will place their own feet. It is often only after you have run your race that you are overwhelmed by the positive impact you have left. In fact, your ability to make positive footprints as a leader in any sphere will be greatly determined by your ability to make positive footprints and make a legacy as a leader's servant. If you do not have a good legacy as a servant, the chances are you will not have a good legacy as a leader.

A faithful servant may find themselves the subject of many biographies written during and after their lifetime, describing them as a history maker by virtue of the good example of servanthood they set.

"Carve your name on hearts, not tombstones. A legacy is etched into the minds of others and the stories they share about you" *(Shannon Adler).*

A faithful servant will become a learning opportunity for many others. They can become a renowned and an acclaimed model for their own generation, the pride of their family and nation.

"That is your legacy on this earth. When you leave this earth, how many hearts have you touched?" (Patti Davis).

7. FULFILMENT OF GOD'S AGENDA

Our faithful servanthood on earth leads to the fulfilment of God's intended agenda for our societies and nations. That fulfilment brings glory to God. It is a great reward and privilege for you to have been instrumental in the service of God's kingdom agenda. To have been chosen to serve in whatever sphere is a privilege and an honour because it means that you were deemed to have what it takes in terms of a potential that simply needed to be unleashed. You ended up being a chosen tool and vessel in God's hands to accomplish His purposes (either in your family, in your nation's leadership and governance, in private or public enterprises, the economy of your nation, the welfare of your society and community or the mission of the Body of Christ).

The fact that you excelled and were counted faithful is a big reward. Your service propels other people to their destiny. For God to deem you worthy of fulfilling His agenda is the highest reward, the greatest affirmation, you could possibly seek for and receive.

Thought Provoking Questions for Discussion

1. Do you know anyone who has been highly honoured and esteemed as a result of their servanthood?

2. Have you ever felt more empowered as a result of serving?

3. Do you believe that personal joy and fulfilment are rewards for servanthood?

4. Is there a desired harvest in your life that you know you received as a result of your servanthood? If so, what was it?

5. Do you know of people who have served faithfully and been recognized? If so, how were they recognized?

6. What kind of legacy do you think you are building as you serve? Do you see it as a reward for your servanthood?

7. How does it make you feel to play a role in fulfilling God's agenda? Will this be enough for you even if there was no other reward?

THE 7 ETERNAL REWARDS (HEAVENLY)

The seven eternal or heavenly rewards are referred to and described in the Bible. Some may be tempted to despise and look down on such rewards because of their seeming distance from where we are right now. A common expression is such things are *"pie in the sky when you die."*

However, faithful servants do not look upon these rewards with cynicism. They regard them as invaluable incentives for serving faithfully because they are not given by fickle human beings who may change their minds any time, promising a reward one minute in order to manipulate you into serving them, then going back on their word the next, when you have done what they wanted.

These eternal rewards are sure and irrevocable because of the nature of the One who is promising them to you. God is faithful to keep His word. He is not a man that He should lie nor the son of man that He should repent. He is a promise keeper who does not break His covenant with us. So, then, what heavenly rewards does he promise the faithful servant on earth?

1. MANSIONS IN HEAVEN

"Let not your heart be troubled; you believe in God, believe also in Me. In My Father's house are many mansions; if it were not so, I would have told you. I go to prepare a place for you. And if I go and prepare a place for you, I will come again and receive you to Myself; that where I am, there you may be also" (John14:1-3)

This is Jesus speaking to His disciples before He ascended into heaven. He was encouraging them that there is a glorious end to their work on earth. There are mansions for them and us in heaven.

2. CROWNS

The Bible speaks of five crowns that a faithful servant will receive as a badge of royalty (1 Corinthians 9:24-25):

An imperishable, incorruptible crown (1 Peter 1:3-5; Matthew 6:19)

A crown of rejoicing (1 Thessalonians 2:19)

A crown of righteousness (2 Timothy 4:8; Philippians 3:20)

A crown of glory (1 Peter 5:4; Romans 8:18; Isaiah 42:8)

A crown of life (Revelation 2:10; John 10:10)

3. ETERNAL LIFE

"Then the King will say to those on His right hand, 'Come, you blessed of My Father, inherit the kingdom prepared for you from the foundation of the world: for I was hungry and you gave Me food; I was thirsty and you gave Me drink; I was a stranger and you took Me in; I was naked and you clothed Me; I was sick and you visited Me; I was in prison and you came to Me'." (Matthew 25:34-36)

We see here a parable about receiving the Kingdom after having served without expecting any reward. Those who fed the hungry, visited the sick and ministered to people in prison all have one thing in common: they served audiences who had no capacity to reward them. God rewards such servanthood with an inheritance – the rule of heaven in the new heavens and new earth.

4. PRAISE

"Nothing else can quite substitute for a few well-chosen, well-timed, sincere words of praise. They're absolutely free and worth a fortune" (Sam Walton).

A faithful servant will receive the praise of their master. The praise of the master leads to open doors and respect from their fellow servants. We read in Genesis 4:3-6:

"And in the process of time it came to pass that Cain brought an offering of the fruit of the ground to the Lord. Abel also brought of the firstborn of his flock and of their fat. And the Lord respected Abel and his offering, but He did not respect Cain and his offering. And Cain was very angry, and his countenance fell. So, the Lord said to Cain, "Why are you angry? And why has your countenance fallen? If you do well, will you not be accepted?"

Doing well earns God's praise. God's praise is a heavenly and eternal reward. It is a potent incentive for faithful service.

5. GOD AS A REWARD

When you serve as unto the Lord, God Himself becomes your reward. Deuteronomy 10:8-9 says, *"At that time the Lord separated the tribe of Levi to bear the ark of the covenant of the Lord, to stand before the Lord to minister to Him and to bless in His name, to this day. Therefore, Levi has no portion nor inheritance with his brethren; the Lord is his inheritance, just as the Lord your God promised him."*

The Levites had God as their reward, and this was enough. This is because when one has God, then one has everything.

We see something similar in the story of Abram in Genesis 15:1: *"After these things the word of the Lord came to Abram in a vision, saying, 'Do not be afraid, Abram. I am your shield, your exceedingly great reward'."*

Abraham had this promise from God, that as he walked blamelessly before the Lord, God would be His reward. As a result, Abraham was one of the most blessed men who ever lived. To this day, we speak of the Abrahamic blessing.

6. PROTECTION

Exodus 23:25-26 says,

"So, you shall serve the Lord your God, and He will bless your bread and your water. And I will take sickness away from the midst of you. No one shall suffer miscarriage or be barren in your land; I will fulfil the number of your days."

From this verse, we see a promise of protection from sickness and barrenness, and a promise of long life as a reward for serving God. Long life means one is protected from premature death from accidents, terror attacks, bandits or natural calamity.

7. ESCAPE TRIBULATION

Revelation 3:10 says, *"Since you have kept my command to endure patiently, I will also keep you from the hour of trial that is going to come on the whole world to test the inhabitants of the earth."*

In our service to the Lord, we may have to endure many things. These may include the temperamental weaknesses of the person we are serving, difficult times in the organization or even false accusations. When we endure patiently and do not waver from the faith, we will be delivered from the ordinary tribulations we face and from the great and final tribulation before Jesus Christ returns.

Thought Provoking Questions for Discussion

1. Do you ever think about eternal rewards as you are serving?

2. Why do you think God gives rewards in heaven?

3. What does God being your reward mean to you?

4. What is the most difficult trial you have had to endure in your service?

5. Can you cite an incident where you know you were preserved because of your service?

6. Have you ever received praise from the person you are serving? How did it make you feel?

7. Have you begun to experience any eternal rewards here on earth?

Conclusion

In conclusion therefore each one of us is a servant and our Servanthood is connected to our destiny Walking in the **7P's of Servanthood** that this book has expounded on is key to our effectiveness.

How we serve will have an impact in our societies and nations whether positively or negatively so if we care for the welfare of our nations and the people in our nations, we will take our service to a higher level and see ourselves and our nations thrive.

The 7P's of Servanthood expounded in the Book entail understanding our **Persona** as we serve, owning and being secure in our self-identity, discovering our **Purpose** and the functions of our Servanthood so that we serve within our mandates, being positioned in our right **Place** of service and taking up our rightful posts there, identifying and collaborating with the **People** who are essential in our Servanthood namely those we are serving and those we are serving with, embracing the **Process** that will mould us and enable us to serve better, walking by the **Principles** upon which our Servanthood is found and being motivated by the **Prize** that awaits us after we have served faithfully.

Bibliography

The Bible

Munroe, Myles. 1992. *Maximizing your potential.* Destiny Image Publishers, Inc. U.S.A

While, Jerry. 1985. The *Power of Commitment: How Ordinary People Can Make an Extraordinary Impact on the World* (Life and Ministry of Jesus Christ). NavPress U.S.A.

Maredith, Martin. 2013. *The State of Africa: A History of the Continent Since Independence.* Simon & Schuster U.K. Press

Kinyanjui, W. Teresa. 2011. A Cactus in the Desert; An Autobiography with Anne Jackson

Collins, Jim. 2001. *Good to Great: Why Some Companies Make the Leap and Others Don't.* HarperCollins Publisher Inc, New York

Collins, Jim.1994. *Built to Last: Successful Habits of Visionary Companies.* HarperCollins Publisher Inc, New York

Adelaja, Sunday. 2008. *Church Shift: Revolutionizing Your Faith, Church, and Life for the 21st Century.*

Enlow, Johnny. 2008. *The Seven Mountain Prophecy: Unveiling the Coming Elijah Revolution.* Thomas Nelson, Inc. Publisher, U.S.A